THE ART OF TEACHING CREATIVE WRITING

A STEP-BY-STEP GUIDE TO TEACH CREATIVE WRITING WITH CONCEPT NOTES, LESSON PLANS, INDUCTION ACTIVITIES AND SAMPLE WORKSHEETS

FOR EDUCATORS, EDUPRENEURS, PARENTS AND LITERATURE LOVERS

PRITI GALA

AF486653

ISBN 979-8-89277-950-0

CONTENTS

WHAT IS CREATIVE WRITING?

When anyone thinks of creative writing, they think compositions, letters, stories etc. That is true to an extent as most of us are exposed to creative writing in school as we learn to write paragraphs, picture stories and so on.

However, Creative Writing goes much beyond the conventional realms and encompasses whole range of expressions using various forms and genres of writing.

It is articulation, eloquence and expression of ideas, thoughts and feelings.

What are the different types of creative writing?

Creative writing comes in many forms, encompassing a number of genres and styles. There are lots of different types of creative writing, which can be categorised as fiction or non-fiction. Some of the most popular being:

- Biographies/Autobiographies
- Fiction: Novels, Novellas, Short Stories, etc
- Non-Fiction: Articles, Reports, Blogs
- Diary writing and Journaling
- Letters and Emails
- Speeches
- Poetry and spoken word
- Playwriting/scriptwriting
- Narrative, Descriptive and Personal essays

In the words of Albert Einstein, "creativity is fun for the intellect," and writing is a great way to help your child express themselves. Statistics show that reading helps develop your writing skills, but writing helps develop your cognitive growth, organizational skills, and the ability to influence others through persuasion.

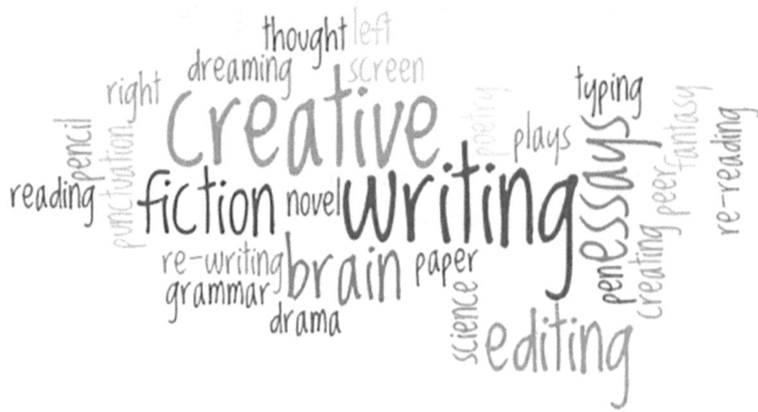

Why Creative Writing is important?

Imagination And Creativity

Creative writing encourages kids to exercise their creative minds and practice using their imaginations. It improves their ability to come up with alternatives. This broadens their thought processes, which can lead to success in many areas, including problem solving and analysis.

Self-Expression

Children often have difficulty understanding and expressing how they feel. Through writing, children have a safe place to explore, and this can be a highly beneficial tool for expressing their feelings.

Self-Confidence

Writing gives children more opportunity to assert themselves and their opinions and develop their "voice." These developments can really strengthen their self-confidence.

Communication And Persuasion Skills

A well-written piece involves a lot of thought, planning, organization, and use of language to get a point across. What great practice for kids at laying out their thoughts and trying to clearly convince someone of their point of view.

Enhances Comprehension skill

Writing forces students to improve reading comprehension skills as well as grammar and vocabulary knowledge. One of the most important things your child can learn in school is how to read.

Exposure to language

It provides an opportunity for students to experiment with different types of words, formats, and sentence structures. It expands their vocabulary and gives them an edge to express more clearly.

Creative writing is not just about forming sentences and paragraphs, but fostering imagination and creative thinking. It inspires kids to write creatively and have fun in the process. By engaging in creative writing your child will develop better observation and perceptive skills and gain confidence.

A child who can articulate, express and communicate eloquently definitely has an advantage in any strata -be it in school or in life.

WHY CREATIVE WRITING

Creative writing is not just about forming sentences and paragraphs, but fostering imagination and creative thinking. It inspires kids to write creatively and have fun in the process. By engaging in creative writing the child will develop better observation and perceptive skills and gain confidence.

A child who can articulate, express and communicate eloquently definitely has an advantage in any strata – be it in school or in life.

> "You should write because you love the shape of stories and sentences and the creation of different words on a page. Writing comes from reading, and reading is the finest teacher of how to write."
>
> Annie Proulx

HELPING TEACHERS TEACH CREATIVE WRITING BETTER: A HANDBOOK FOR INSPIRING STORIES

Teaching how to write creatively can be like guiding a journey into a magical world of words. Imagine having a special guidebook for teachers to help them lead students on this exciting adventure. That's exactly what the Creative Writing Teacher's Handbook is all about!

This special book is like a treasure chest for teachers. It's filled with great ideas and easy-to-follow plans that help teachers teach creative writing in fun and exciting ways. You know, like games and activities that make writing feel like an amazing adventure.

Why did I make this handbook? Well, turns out, there weren't many books like this around. Teachers often didn't have a special guide just for teaching creative writing. So, I decided to make one to help them become even better at what they do.

This handbook is like having a team of expert teachers sharing their best secrets. I gathered lots of clever ideas and methods from various sources who are really good at inspiring young writers. Their experiences and smart ideas are now part of this book! I have added all my insights and what has worked in my classroom in these many years of teaching creative writing to kids.

But why is this handbook so important? Because it helps teachers make writing lessons super interesting! When teachers have exciting ways to teach, students get more excited too. And that's when magic happens—students start loving writing, coming up with fantastic stories,essays etc!

It provides a coherence, step by step guide on how to teach creative writing. What tools to use and how to give children the thought process to do creative writing.

This book is not just about teaching; it's about creating a happy space for learning. It's like giving teachers a guide/a handbook to make writing classes awesome for kids everywhere.

So, this handbook isn't just a book—it's like a special map guiding teachers on an adventure to discover the amazing world of creative writing with their students. Together, they'll create stories that sparkle and words that dance off the pages!

1. <u>Educational Resource:</u> It provides a comprehensive guide for teachers who aim to nurture and develop their students' creative writing skills. It becomes a resource that offers techniques, exercises, and methodologies to enhance teaching effectiveness.
2. <u>Filling a Gap:</u> Often, there is a lack of consolidated resources specifically tailored to teaching creative writing. This handbook fills this gap by offering a structured and comprehensive approach.
3. <u>Sharing Expertise:</u> It has helped me to share your expertise, insights, and experiences in the field of creative writing education. My unique perspective and methods can benefit other educators seeking guidance.
4. <u>Empowering Teachers:</u> By equipping teachers with effective strategies and tools, the handbook empowers them to inspire and guide students in discovering their creative potential.
5. <u>Impact on Students:</u> Ultimately, the aim is to positively impact students' learning experiences. A well-crafted handbook helps teachers engage students more effectively, encouraging them to explore their creativity and improve their writing skills.

6. <u>Community Contribution:</u> Contributing to the educational community by sharing best practices, innovative ideas, and successful teaching methods fosters collaboration and growth among educators.

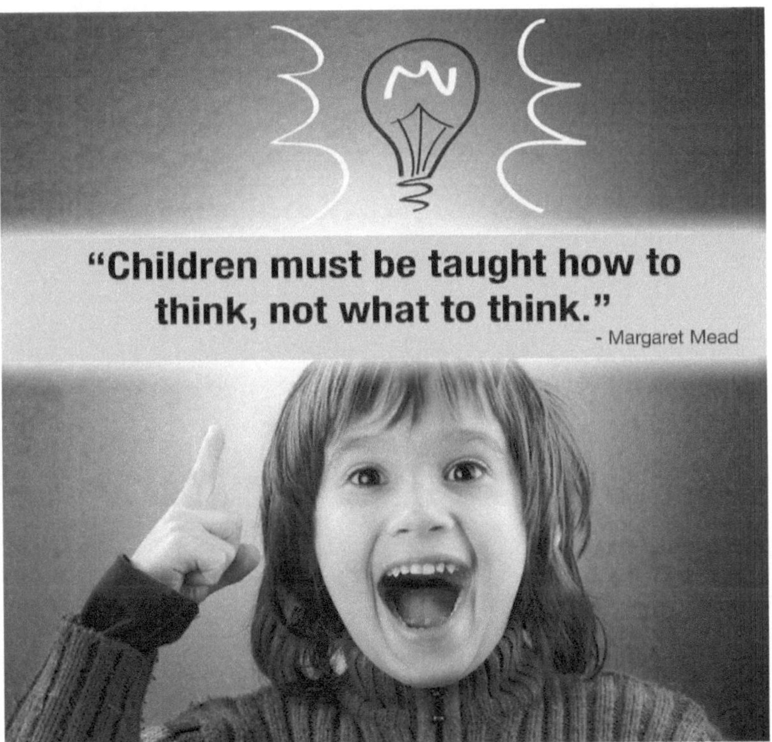

What will you get in these pages:

Every chapter has

> **Essential concepts,**
> **Comprehensive lesson plans,**
> **Engaging induction activities ideas, enriched vocabulary banks,**
> **Remarkable sample writings (mostly by my students) and**
> **Diverse question banks that teachers can use in their classroom.**

CHAPTER 1

BLAH TO BRILLIANT

1.1 Introduction:

Words are the building blocks of human expression. They have the remarkable ability to shape our thoughts, convey our emotions, and ignite our imaginations.

Using appropriate and interesting words makes your writing more vivid and descriptive. It is necessary to use words that convey the intended meaning.

The concept is of taking 'blah' words, the mundane and ordinary, and elevating them to 'brilliant' words, the extraordinary and evocative.

Blah to Brilliant words!

Blah	Brilliant
Angry	Annoyed, Enraged, Furious, Irritated, Indignant
Bad	Appalling, Awful, Depressed, Gloomy, Dejected
Beautiful	Attractive, Enchanting, Delightful, Enchanting, Gorgeous
Big	Ample, Colossal, Gigantic, Enormous, Magnificent, Humongous
Cruel	Brutal, Heartless, Harsh, Cold-Blooded

Good	Pleasant, Awesome, Amazing, Delightful, Excellent
Happy	Blithe, Cheerful, Blissful, Ecstatic, Exhilarated, Exuberant
Hot	Fiery, Scorching, Scalding, Sultry, Burning
Honest	Candid, Faithful, Righteous, Sincere, Upright
Intelligent	Astute, Brainy, Gifted, Erudite, Quick-Witted
Lazy	Slouch, Sluggish, Couch-Potato, Lazybones, Lethargic
Great	Astounding, Breath-Taking, Dazzling, Remarkable
Sad	Dismal, Dejected, Cheerless, Depressed, Grim, Woeful, Pensive
Small	Atomic, Bite-Sized, Dwarfish, Negligible, Trivial
Strong	Brawny, Infallible, Muscular, Virulent, Indefatigable
Ugly	Horrid, Grotesque, Abhorrent, Obnoxious

Examples:

A. Nouns:

1. Words for Courage

Guts	Stability	Resolved	Unafraid	Brave
Mettle	Readiness	Self Confidence	Zeal	Patience

2. Words for Hate

Abhor	Grievance	Disfavour	Ire	Dislike
Foul	Hound	Deprecate	Miff	Mourn

3. Words for Laughter Or Amusement

Chaff	Rag	Smirk	Snigger	Put-Down
Dig	Droll	Taunt	Teasing	Jab

4. Words for Light

Bright	Sunny	Flashy	Glowing	Brilliant
Aflame	Shining	Blinding	Flaring	Radiant

5. Words for Pain

Ache	Agony	Ceaseless Pain	Mild Pain	Sorrow
Burning Pain	Acute Pain	Crippling Pain	Hurt	Sting

6. Words for Pleasure

Amusement	Distraction	Joy	Elation	Seemly
Thrill	Satisfaction	Happiness	Fun	Bliss

7. Words for Speed

Abrupt	Zoom	In a flash		
Breakneck	Tempo	Unending		

8. Words for Friend

Companion	Ally	Confidant	Comrade	Amigo
Kindred Spirit				

9. Words for Home

Residence	Abode	Dwelling	Heaven	Sanctum
Domicile				

10. Words for Love

Affection	Adoration	Devotion	Passion	Affinity
Intimacy	Amorous	Rapture		

B. Verbs:

1. Words for Cry

Bawl	Weep	Grizzle	Wail	Teary
Groan	Sob	Moan	Howl	

2. Words for Eat

Bite	Gulp	Gobble	Taste	Peck
Drink	Sip	Swallow	Stuff	Munch

3. Words for Get

Acquire	Beg	Buy	Grab	Wrest
Find	Gain	Profit	Obtain	

4. Words for Like

Admire	Adore	Care for	Adulation for	Approve of
Appreciate	Cherish			

5. Words for Look

Appear	Ogle	Skim	Scan	Survey
Witness	Gawp	View	See	

6. Words for Walk

Advance	Frisk	Trek	Trot	Wobble
Saunter	Amble	Stride	Skip	Trudge

More verbs:

1. Talk: Speak, Chat, Converse, Articulate
2. Run: Jog, Sprint, Dash, Race
3. See: Observe, Notice, Glimpse, Behold
4. Read: Scan, Peruse, Devour, Absorb
5. Write: Compose, Craft, Pen, Create
6. Feel: Sense, Perceive, Experience, Empathize
7. Sleep: Doze, Slumber, Nap, Rest
8. Love: Adore, Cherish, Idolize, Worship

C. Adjectives:

1. Words for Angry

Annoyed	Mad	Wild	Livid	Irate
Savage	Violent	Cross	Raging	Incensed

2. Words for Arrogant

Upstart	Aloof	Superior	Haughty	Overbearing
Vain	Proud	Snooty	Insulting	Lordly

3. Words for Bad

Dangerous	Faulty	Hazardous	Naughty	Unfit
Dingy	Gloomy	Shameless	Rude	Stale

4. Words for Beautiful

Attractive	Charming	Wonderful	Stunning	Good-looking
Lovely	Superb	Pretty	Handsome	Flawless

5. Words for Big

Ample	Giant	Jumbo	Heavy	Giant
Burly	Husky	King Size	Massive	Comprehensive

6. Words for Cold

Icy	Chilly	Frosty	Thumping	Freezing
Bitter	Frozen	Sub-zero	Wintry	Glacial

7. Words for Cowardly

Chicken	Timid	Craven	Toothless	Limp
Shaky	Floppy	Frail	Puny	Gutless

8. Words for Cruel

Vile	Mean	Unkind	Inhuman	Evil
Nasty	Savage	Wolfish	Criminal	Harsh

9. Words for Cunning

Canny	Sly	Wily	Craft	Slick
Glib	Clever	Foxy	Oily	Calculating

10. Words for Dishonest

Unfair	False	Lying	Cheat	Dishonourable
Misleading	Corrupt	Venal	Underhand	Untruthful

11. Words for Dry

Arid	Thirsty	Parched	Wrinkled	Dehydrated
Drought	Barren	Waterless	Shrunken	Withered

12. Words for Good

Able	Clear	Helpful	Super	Useful
Pleasant	Expert	Moral	Safe	Fine

13. Words for Happy

Smiling	Radiant	Aglow	Sunny	Blissful
Cherry	Merry	Glad	Joyful	Excited

14. Words for Honest

Fair	Rely	Moral	Clean	Holy
Honourable	Sincere	Pure	Frank	Good

15. Words for Hot

Muggy	Boiling	Torrid	Intense	Burning
Searing	Fiery	Sizzling	Melting	Sultry

16. Words for Innocent

Artless	Unworldly	Safe	Sinless	Naïve
Open	Simple	worthy	Truthful	Uncorrupted

17. Words for Intelligent

Able	Smart	Thinking	Sensible	Bright
Clever	Quick	Wise	Logical	Rational

18. Words for Lazy

Bask	Bum	Slouch	Kill time	Lazybones
Lie	Loll around	Hang around	Shirker	Loafer

19. Words for Nice

Pure	Kind	Delicate	Correct	Polite
Sugary	Fine	Good-Looking	Tame	Sensitive

20. Words for Pain

Ache	Agony	Ceaseless Pain	Mild Pain	Sorrow
Burning Pain	Acute Pain	Crippling Pain	Hurt	Sting

21. Words for Pleasure

Amusement	Distraction	Joy	Elation	Seemly
Thrill	Satisfaction	Happiness	Fun	Bliss

22. Words for Plenty

Abundant	Considerable	Loads	Bounty	Extensive
Heaps	Liberal	Ample	Lavish	Greatly

23. Words for Great

Amazing	Wonderful	Excellent	Mind-Blowing	Dazzling
Awesome	Unbelievable	Stunning	Unique	Fabulous

24. Words for Restless

Agitated	On Edge	Active	Restless	Restive
Edgy	Hyper	Anxious	Uneasy	Nervous

25. Words for Rough

Edgy	Agitated	Uneven	Gruff	Restive
On Edge	Shifty	Stubby	Restless	Nervous

26. Words for Sad

Blue	Sorry	Dark	Worrying	Unhappy
Dingy	Pitiful	Dismal	Down	Moving

27. Words for Scared

Afraid	Awe-Struck	Cower	Worried	Recoil
Fearful	Nervous	Panic	Wince	Dread

28. Words for Sick

Balked	Ill	Fainted	Sweating	Unwell
Choking	Bleeding	Vomit	Uneasy	Shaking

29. Words for Small

Atomic	Tiny	Speck	Titbit	Nano
Minor	Midget	Teeny	Wee	Crumb

30. Words for Stingy

Mean	Grudging	Ungenerous	Miserly	Tightfisted
Miserly	Penny - Pinching	Scrimpy	Sparing	Parsimonious

31. Words for Strange

Abnormal	Freaky	Unusual	Unnatural	New
Different	Irregular	Queer	Unfamiliar	Rare

32. Words for Strong

Beefy	Secure	Solid	Robust	Firm
Build To Last	Stoic	Tough	Unafraid	Burly

33. Words for Stubborn

Adamant	Intractable	Obstinate	Unbendable	Grim
Dogged	Implacable	Relentless	Unwavering	Rigid

34. Words for Stupid

Dull	Silly	Rash	Brainless	Inane
Witless	Thick	Futile	Foolish	Idiotic

35. Words for Timid

Withdrawn	Timorous	Nervous	Diffident	Mousy
Quiet	Wary	Tentative	Bashful	Shy

36. Words for Wet

Damp	Soaking	Watery	Soaked	Moist
Icy	Rainy	Wave	Wet Through	Foggy

37. Words for Worried

Tense	Bothered	Stressed	Sick	Nervous
Pensive	Disturbed	Unhappy	Vexed	Unbalanced

38. Words for Lonely

Lost	Deserted	Unsocial	Bereft	Remote
Hermit	Cut Off	Sole	Recluse	Unwanted

39. Words for Bold

Audacious	Daring	Courageous	Intrepid	Adventurous
Fearless	Gutsy	Unflinching	Dauntless	Resolute

40. Words for Glowing

Luminous	Incandescent	Resplendent	Dazzling	Illuminated
Ablaze	Radiating	Shimmering	Gleaming	Vibrant

1.2 Lesson Plan/Induction activities:

The best way to teach children good vocabulary is to demonstrate it by using it as a teacher. They will learn it fast in that manner.

To teach brilliant vocabulary, the teacher can adopt various methods in the classroom.

1. Have a general conversation, where you ask children to replace common words like good, nice etc with more appropriate and descriptive words. So, if you ask children how their weekend was?

If responses are mundane 'good', 'nice', 'bad' etc. Explain them they can be more articulate if they use words such as interesting, amazing, boring, hectic etc.

2. Show sample texts. Create your own or take from literature texts to show the use of brilliant vocabulary.

A. The **luminous** sun cast a golden glow over the **tranquil** lake, where the water **shimmered** like a field of scattered diamonds.

B. Lucy, their **inspiring** teacher, stood before the **captivated** students. "Today, we'll explore our very own enchanted forest," she announced.

Sarah, the class's **imaginative** storyteller, raised her hand. "Miss Lucy, can I be an explorer in the forest?"

"Of course, Sarah," Lucy replied, her eyes **sparkling with enthusiasm**. "Jake, what role would you like?"

Jake, the quiet yet **thoughtful** boy, hesitated before saying, "I want to be a forest guide, helping everyone find hidden treasures."

1.3 Sample Worksheets:

A. In the following sentences, change the blah words to brilliant words.

1. The pizza tasted bad.

   ____

2. The weather looked sad which made Anne even more sad.

   ____

3. The little spring of the plant sprouted up in the corner of the wall.

   ____

4. The princess was wearing a beautiful tiara.

   ____

5. Little John was scared of the frog.

   ____

6. The clown was making funny faces.

   ____

7. My day was good!

   ____

8. The quiet library was filled with books.

   ____

9. The sleepy baby cuddled with a soft blanket.

   ____

10. The fast car zoomed down the dusty road.

   ____

B. Classify the following words in Blah and Brilliant.

> Sad, dreadful, dazzling, bad, beautiful, happy, obnoxious, muscular, brutal, good, elated, lazy, astounding, great

Blah	Brilliant

C. Give two brilliant words for each blah word and make sentences using those brilliant words.

1. Bad

    First word - _______________________________

    Sentence - _______________________________

    Second word - _______________________________

    Sentence - _______________________________

2. Honest

    First word - _______________________________

    Sentence - _______________________________

    Second word - _______________________________

    Sentence - _______________________________

3. Angry

    First word - _______________________________

    Sentence - _______________________________

    Second word - _______________________________

    Sentence - _______________________________

4. Happy

    First word - _______________________________

    Sentence - _______________________________

Second word - ______________________________

Sentence - ____

5. Strong

First word - _____________________________

Sentence - ____

Second word - ______________________________

Sentence - ____

1.4 Sample Literature References:

1. Here's a passage from Lemony Snicket's "A Series of Unfortunate Events: The Reptile Room" that showcases a brilliant use of vocabulary:

"In the centre of the room, high atop a long pole, hung a chandelier, a **colossal** chandelier, and the word colossal, here, means very, very, very, very large. In fact, the chandelier was so **enormous**, and its crystals so numerous and **dazzling**, that it is a **miracle** it did not **plummet** to the floor."

1. Here's a passage from J.K. Rowling's "Harry Potter and the Half-Blood Prince" that demonstrates her brilliant vocabulary:

"The sun was barely visible over the horizon as he **gazed** across the sea; the morning was quiet except for a gull that **swooped** low over the water and the **rhythmic clapping** of the waves against the rocks."

1.5 Links for references/ video links:

Vocabulary and writing

https://www.time4writing.com/articles-about-writing/vocabulary/

https://wordcounter.net/blog/2014/01/22/1027_25-ways-to-improve-your-writing-vocabulary.html

https://www.teachwriting.org/612th/2019/7/13/5-ways-to-incorporate-vocabulary-in-writing

https://www.readingandwritinghaven.com/5-brain-based-vocabulary-activities-for-the-secondary-classroom/

https://k12.thoughtfullearning.com/blogpost/12-vocabulary-activities-high-school

CHAPTER 2

DIGGING DEEPER

2.1 Introduction:

Digging deeper- Stretch the sentence.

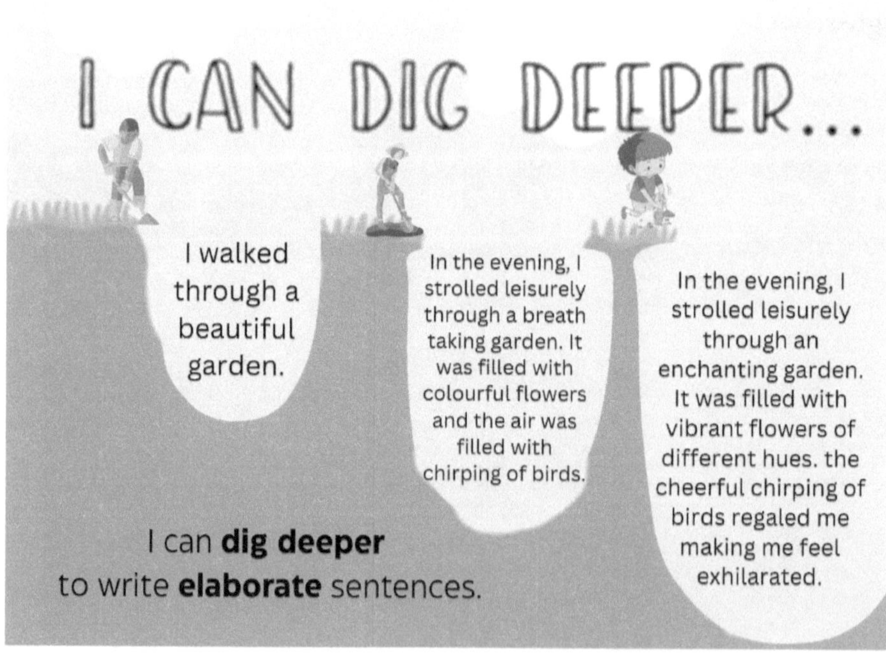

In creative expression and writing, we can dig deeper into our narratives by asking a set of questions that start with "Wh": Who, What, When, Where, and Why.

These questions help us explore and give more details of our characters, plot, setting, and motivations. By using them, we can bring more richness and depth to our narratives. In this chapter, we'll learn how to use these questions effectively to enhance our creative work.

Add more details to give complete and required information.

> ➤ Add adjectives and adverbs.
> ➤ Answer all the Wh and How questions.

For Example-

What – The balloon man sold balloons.

Where – The balloon man sold the balloons **in the fair.**

When – The balloon man sold the balloons **the whole day** in the fair.

Why – The balloon man sold the balloons the whole day in the fair **to make some money for his family.**

How – (generally an adverb or adverb phrase)– The balloon man sold the balloons **cheerfully** the whole day in the fair to make some money for his family.

Add adjectives – The balloon man sold the **colourful, rainbow-like** balloons the whole day in the **temple f**air to make some money for his family.

Examples:

1. Original sentence: WE STOOD OUTSIDE FOR TWENTY MINUTES.

Adjective: We stood outside for twenty <u>miserable</u> minutes.

When: <u>This morning,</u> we stood outside for twenty miserable minutes.

Where: This morning, we stood <u>on the sidewalk in front of the school</u> for twenty miserable minutes.

How: This morning, we <u>stood shivering</u> on a snow covered sidewalk in front of the school for twenty miserable minutes.

Why: This morning, we stood shivering on a snow covered sidewalk in front of the school for twenty miserable minutes <u>waiting for the school bus.</u>

2. Original Sentence: She ran through the park.

Adjective: She ran through the park cheerfully.

When: Yesterday, she ran through the park cheerfully.

Where: Yesterday, she ran through the colourful park cheerfully.

How: Yesterday, she ran through the colourful park cheerfully, feeling the soft grass beneath her feet.

Why: Yesterday, she ran through the colourful park cheerfully, feeling the soft grass beneath her feet, to celebrate her friend's birthday.

In this example, we start with a simple sentence and progressively add details by answering the "Wh" questions, making the narrative more vivid and engaging.

3. Original Sentence: They sang a song.

Adjective: They sang a beautiful song.

When: Last night, they sang a beautiful song.

Where: Last night, they sang a beautiful song by the campfire.

How: Last night, they sang a beautiful song by the crackling campfire, harmonizing with voices that filled the night air.

Why: Last night, they sang a beautiful song by the crackling campfire, harmonizing with voices that filled the night air, to celebrate their friendship and the memories they had made.

WH- HOW

It's the fundamental, the basic

Wh and HOW

What, When, Where, Why, How

Introduce as a story/ Comparative text/ probing question

2.2 Lesson Plan/Induction Activities:

Writing Elaborate Sentences and Paragraphs Using "Wh-" and "How" Questions

Objective:

Students will learn how to use "Wh-" (What, When, Where, Why, Who) and "how" questions to create more detailed and elaborate sentences and paragraphs.

Materials:

- ➢ Whiteboard and markers
- ➢ Projector or handouts with examples
- ➢ Writing materials for students (notebooks or paper)

Introduction (10 minutes):

- ➢ Start by explaining to students that asking questions can help them create more detailed and elaborate sentences and paragraphs.
- ➢ Introduce the concept of "Wh-" questions (What, When, Where, Why, Who) and "how" questions and their role in gathering information.
- ➢ Emphasize that these questions can be used as a framework to add depth and detail to their writing.

Activity 1: Sentence Expansion (15 minutes):

➢ Provide students with a simple sentence, such as "The cat sat on the chair."

➢ Ask students to take turns asking and answering "Wh-" and "how" questions about the sentence. For example:

➢ What colour is the cat?

➢ Where is the chair located?

➢ Why is the cat sitting there?

➢ As students ask questions, encourage them to use their answers to expand the original sentence into a more elaborate one.

➢ Write down the expanded sentences on the board to illustrate the concept.

Activity 2: Paragraph Expansion (15 minutes):

➢ Provide students with a short paragraph that lacks detail, such as "I went to the park."

➢ In pairs or small groups, have students generate "Wh-" and "how" questions about the paragraph to gather more information.

➢ Encourage students to use their questions and answers to expand the paragraph into a more detailed and elaborate description of the park visit.

➢ Ask each group to share their expanded paragraphs with the class.

Conclusion (5 minutes):

Summarize the importance of asking "Wh-" and "how" questions to add depth and detail to writing.

Encourage students to use this technique in their future writing assignments to make their sentences and paragraphs more engaging and informative.

Homework (optional): Assign a writing task where students must write a paragraph about a personal experience, incorporating "Wh-" and "how" questions to make their writing more elaborate.

Like-'How I spent my weekend'

Comparative Text

Example 1- I went to the beach on Sunday Morning.

Example 2- "One sunny morning, I decided to visit the beach. I was curious about what the beach looked like on that day. As I reached the shore, I noticed the sandy shore stretching endlessly and meeting the sparkling waves. The breeze moved the palm trees, and it made me feel peaceful. I considered the timing for a visit, and mornings like these, with fewer people around and a warm sun, are my favourite. I also thought about who enjoys this place, and I saw families building sandcastles, couples walking hand in hand, and surfers catching waves. Lastly, I pondered what made me so fortunate to live near such a beautiful place. Moments like these make me appreciate the simple joys of life, and I couldn't help but smile as I walked along the shore."

2.3 Sample Worksheets:

A. Dig deeper and stretch the following sentences-

1. The little child was crying.

What – ______________________________

When – ______________________________

Where – ______________________________

Why – ______________________________

How – ______________________________

2. Girls were making garlands.

What – _______________________________

When –_______________________________

Where – _______________________________

Why – _______________________________

How – _______________________________

3. Teacher taught us the lesson.

What – _______________________________

When –_______________________________

Where – _______________________________

Why – _______________________________

How – _______________________________

4. The birds were singing.

What – _______________________________

When –_______________________________

Where – _______________________________

Why – _______________________________

How – _______________________________

5. We went walking.

What – _______________________________

When – _______________________________

Where – _______________________________

Why – _______________________________

How – _______________________________

B. Digging Deeper-

1. The cat slept in the basket.

____

____

____

____

____

2. The baker baked a cake

____

____

____

____

____

3. The travellers were tired.

____

____

____

____

____

4. The storyteller narrated a tale.

____

____

____

____

____

ADDING ADJECTIVES

3.1 Introduction:

- Adjectives are describing words which describe the nouns. Adjectives talk about the shape, size, colour, quality of nouns. Adjectives are like little gems that bring life and colour to our writing.
- Examples of Adjectives: Beautiful, brave, fluffy, enormous, delicious
- Using adjectives in creative writing helps paint a picture in the reader's mind, making the story come alive.

- For Example:

    1. Simple Sentence: The cat meowed.
        Adjectives: The small, black, and fluffy cat meowed.
    2. Simple Sentence: The mountain stood.
        Adjectives: The towering, majestic, and snow-capped mountain stood.
    3. Simple Sentence: The river flowed.
        Adjectives: The winding, tranquil, and crystal-clear river flowed.
    4. Simple Sentence: The cake smelled.
        Adjectives: The sweet, chocolatey, and freshly-baked cake smelled.
    5. Simple Sentence: The house creaked.
        Adjectives: The old, wooden, and eerie house creaked.

The RULE OF 3 should be followed while adding adjectives.

An adjective tells you more about the:

1. Quantity: Few, many, several, ample, myriad
2. Size: Large, small, enormous, petite, colossal
3. Shape: Square, round, triangular, oval, hexagonal
4. Colour: Red, blue, green, yellow, indigo
5. Texture: Smooth, rough, silky, gritty, velvety
6. Age: Young, old, modern, antique, contemporary
7. Origin: Italian, Japanese, ancient, local, foreign
8. Quality: Excellent, poor, exceptional, subpar, flawless
9. Characteristic: Wooden, ceramic, metallic, organic, synthetic

Examples:

Here's a list of adjective-noun combinations that you can provide to students as a "bank" for various creative writing exercises:

1. Sparkling stars
2. Mysterious forest

3. Gigantic waves
4. Whispering wind
5. Bursting fireworks
6. Enchanted castle
7. Gleaming treasure
8. Soothing music
9. Ancient ruins
10. Velvet night
11. Delicious aroma
12. Radiant sunrise
13. Silent footsteps
14. Huge waterfall
15. Lush garden
16. Fiery sunset
17. Crackling campfire
18. Crisp autumn leaves
19. Gentle snowfall
20. Eerie silence

3.2 Lesson Plan/ Induction activity:

Lesson Plan: The Importance of Adjectives in Creative Writing

Objective:

➢ Students will understand the role of adjectives in creative writing.
➢ Students will be able to use adjectives effectively to enhance their creative writing.

Materials:

➢ Whiteboard and markers
➢ Slides or handouts with examples
➢ A short creative writing prompt for a class activity
➢ List of adjectives (for activity 1)

Introduction (10 minutes):

➢ Begin by asking students if they know what adjectives are and where they have seen or heard them before.

➢ Define adjectives: words that describe or modify nouns and pronouns.

➢ Explain the importance of adjectives in creative writing, such as making descriptions more vivid and engaging.

Activity 1: Charades with Adjectives (15 minutes):

➢ Divide the class into small groups or pairs.

➢ Provide each group with a list of adjectives (e.g., colourful, fluffy, shiny, mysterious, etc.).

➢ Ask each student to choose their favourite object (e.g., a toy, a book, a piece of clothing) and describe it using the adjectives from the list.

➢ Have one student from each group act out their chosen object while the other students guess what it is based on the description.

➢ After each round, discuss how adjectives made the descriptions more interesting and helped others guess the object.

Activity 2: Adjective Showcase (10 minutes):

➢ Show a slide or handout with a simple sentence like "The cat sat on the chair."

➢ Ask students to suggest adjectives to make the sentence more descriptive (e.g., "The fluffy cat sat on the old, creaky chair.").

➢ Discuss how the added adjectives paint a clearer picture in the reader's mind.

➢ You can add more sentence examples to demonstrate.

Activity 3: Creative Writing Prompt (10 minutes):

➢ Provide a creative writing prompt, such as "Write a short paragraph about a park/ mysterious forest."(Depending on the grade)

➤ Ask students to write their paragraphs, emphasizing the use of adjectives to make their descriptions vivid and engaging.
➤ Encourage them to share their paragraphs with the class or in small groups.

Conclusion (5 minutes):

➤ Summarize the importance of adjectives in creative writing.
➤ Encourage students to continue using adjectives in their writing to make it more interesting and captivating.
➤ Mention that writers often revise and edit their work to add or improve adjectives for better storytelling.

3.3 Bank:

A. Abandoned Able Absolute Academic Acceptable Acclaimed Accomplished Accurate Aching Acidic Acrobatic

B. Babyish Back Bad Baggy Bare Barren Basic Beautiful Belated Beloved Bizarre

C. Calculating Calm Candid Canine Capital Carefree Careful Careless Caring Cautious

D. Damaged Damp Dangerous Dapper Daring Dark Darling Dazzling Dead Deadly

E. Each Eager Early Earnest Easy Easy-Going Ecstatic Edible Educated Elaborate

F. Fabulous Failing Faint Fair Faithful Fake False Familiar Famous Fancy

G. Gargantuan Gaseous General Generous Gentle Genuine Giant Giddy Gifted Gigantic

H. Hairy Half Handmade Handsome Handy Happy Happy-Go-Lucky Hard Harsh Healthy

I. Ideal Idle Ignorant Ill Illegal Imaginary Impressive Incompetent Incomplete Inconsistent

J. Jealous Jittery Jolly Joyous Jubilant Jaunty Joking Just Jovial

K. Keen Kind Knowledgeable Kingly

L. Lazy Light Lively Lonely Long Lovely Lucky

M. Magnificent Misty Modern Motionless Muddy Mushy Mysterious

N. Nasty Naughty Nervous Nice Nutty Noble Nurturing Nonchalant Notable Nutritious Nimble

O. Obedient Obnoxious Odd Old-Fashioned Open Outrageous Outstanding

P. Panicky Perfect Plain Pleasant Poised Poor Powerful

Q. Quaint Qualified Quick Quiet Quotable Quantitative Quenching Quivering

R. Real Relieved Repulsive Rich Remarkable Resilient Resolute Resourceful Respectful Rustic Radiant Ravishing

S. Scary Selfish Shiny Shy Silly Sleepy Smiling Smoggy Sore Sparkling Splendid Spotless Stormy Strange Stupid Successful Super

T. Talented Tame Tasty Tender Tense Terrible Thankful Thoughtful Thoughtless Tired Tough Troubled

U. Ugliest Ugly Uninterested Unsightly Unusual Upset Uptight

V. Vast Victorious Vivacious

W. Wandering Weary Wicked Wide-Eyed Wild Witty Worried Worrisome Wrong

X. Xenophobic

Y. Young Youthful

Z. Zany Zealous

3.4 Sample Worksheets:

A. Think of at least five adjectives for the words given below:

1. Rabbit:

__________ __________ __________ __________ __________

2. Magician:

__________ __________ __________ __________ __________

3. Doorbell:

__________ __________ __________ __________ __________

4. Lady:

__________ __________ __________ __________ __________

5. School:

__________ __________ __________ __________ __________

6. Story:

__________ __________ __________ __________ __________

7. Leaf:

__________ __________ __________ __________ __________

8. Dog:

__________ __________ __________ __________ __________

9. Flower:

__________ __________ __________ __________ __________

10. Bird:

__________ __________ __________ __________ __________

B. Complete these sentences with adjectives for your friend. Be as descriptive as possible:

1. This is my __________ friend __________.
2. She is __________ years old.
3. She has got __________ hair and __________ eyes.
4. She has got a __________ nose and a __________ mouth.
5. She loves to wear __________.
6. Her favourite colours are __________ and __________.
7. She is __________ and __________, but sometimes she is __________.
8. She is a __________ girl, and is more __________ than me at school.

C. Complete these sentences with adjectives for your pet cat. Be as descriptive as possible:

1. This is my pet cat and its name is __________.
2. She is __________ in colour and __________ years.
3. She has got a __________ head and two __________ eyes.
4. She has got __________ ears, a __________ nose and a __________ mouth.
5. She has got __________ legs and a very __________ tail/
6. My pet cat can __________, __________ and __________.
7. She is a __________ cat, but sometimes she is __________.
8. She loves to eat __________ and __________.

D. Compose two to three sentences with adjectives for the objects given below:

1. _______________________________

____

____

2. _______________________________

____

____

3. _______________________________

____

____

4. _______________________________

____

____

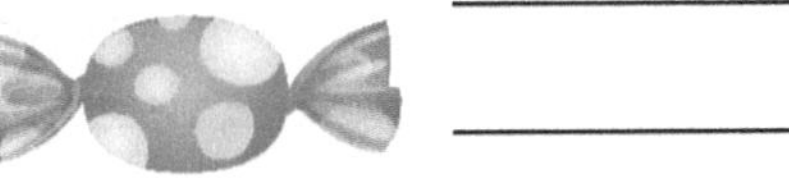

5. _______________________________

____

____

FIGURATIVE LANGUAGE IN WRITING

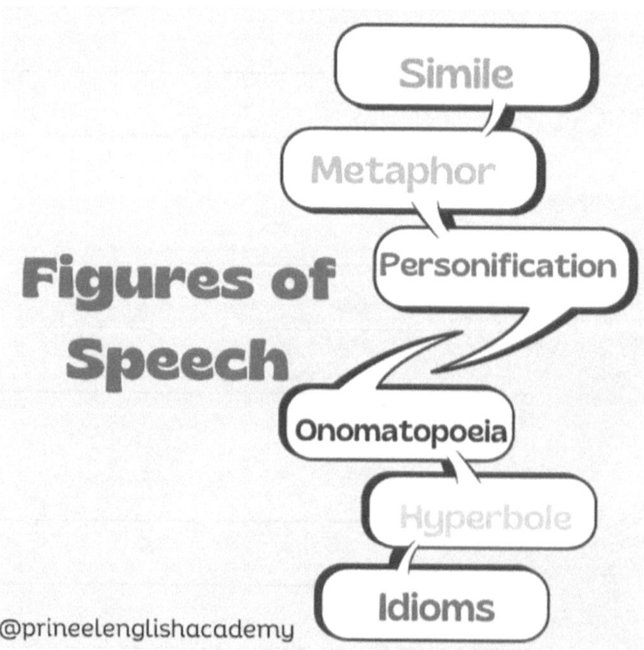

4.1 Introduction:

Figures of speech are rhetorical devices or language techniques used to enhance and convey meaning in a non-literal way. They include various forms of expression such as metaphors, similes, personification, hyperbole, and more, to create vivid and imaginative language that adds depth and color to written or spoken communication.

Types:

A. Based on sound:

1. <u>Alliteration</u> is the term given to the repetition of the same sound or letter at the beginning of words in a phrase.

For example: "Peter **p**icked a **p**eck of **p**ickled **p**eppers" repeats the letter *p*

2. <u>Repetition</u> is a literary device **in which a word or phrase is repeated two or more times.** It is used to make an idea clearer and more memorable.

For example: **Down and down,** went the umbrella.

The boy was a good **footballer,** because his father was a **footballer.**

3. <u>Onomatopoeia</u> is a figure of speech in which words evoke the actual sound of the thing they refer to or describe. An onomatopoeia is a word that sounds the same or similar to the sound it is trying to describe. Onomatopoeia is a kind of descriptive writing that helps bring your work to life.

For example: The "boom" of a firework exploding, the "tick tock" of a clock, and the "dingdong" of a doorbell are all examples of onomatopoeia.

Sound Vocabulary

Ahem	Beep	Blast	Blabber	Buzz
Chirp	Cackle	Chatter	Clash	Cough
Explode	Flutter	Gasp	Giggle	Gaggle
Hiss	Howl	Laugh	Mumble	Moan
Shush	Shriek	Screech	Snore	Thud
Whimper	Whisper	Whistle	Whine	Zoom

B. Based on Similarity:

<u>1. Simile</u> – A simile is a phrase, or group of words, which compares two things using 'like' or 'as'.

Example: 1. Radha and Seema are <u>like peas in a pod.</u>

2. The sage was <u>as wise as an owl.</u>

3. The pen was <u>as light as a feather.</u>

Adding Similes

A simile is a direct comparison of two dissimilar objects using the words 'like' or 'as'.

Example:

His ears were as big as lotus leaves.

Two objects- ears and lotus leaves

Common quality/similarity- big

Her hair looked like flowing waves of the ocean.

Two objects- hair and waves

Common quality/similarity- flowing

How to make a simile-

Take a word such as a 'girl'

Was the girl intelligent/pretty/rude?

If we choose pretty, ask pretty as what?

What else is pretty?

A picture? A flower? A peacock?

Therefore, we make a simile- The girl is as pretty as a flower/ rose.

2. Metaphor: It is a figure of speech that states that one thing *is* another thing. It's used to make a comparison between two objects or concepts that aren't alike but have something in common. It is formed Without using comparative words, such as *like* or *as*.

There are many common examples of metaphors

His heart of stone surprised me.

Time is money.

No man is an island.

- Laughter is the best medicine.

3. Personification: It is a figure of speech in which an idea or thing is given human attributes and/or feelings or is spoken of as if it were human.

Here are some examples of personification:

The sign on the door insulted my intelligence.

My phone is not cooperating with me today.

My computer works very hard.

I like onions, but onions don't like me.

4.2 Lesson Plan/Induction Activities:

Title: Exploring Figurative Language in Creative Writing

Objective: Students will understand and be able to use similes, personification, alliteration, and onomatopoeia effectively in their creative writing.

Materials:

- ➢ Whiteboard and markers or chalkboard and chalk
- ➢ Handouts with examples of similes, personification, alliteration, and onomatopoeia
- ➢ Creative writing prompts or worksheets
- ➢ Art supplies (optional, for visual aids)

Lesson Plan:

Introduction to Figurative Language

Engage (15 minutes): Begin by asking students if they've ever heard phrases like "as busy as a bee" or "the wind whispered through the trees." Explain that these are examples of figurative language, which is a way of making writing more interesting and vivid. Tell students that today, they will learn about four types of figurative language: similes, personification, alliteration, and onomatopoeia.

Explore (15 minutes): Introduce each type of figurative language one by one, providing clear definitions and examples for each:

Similes: Comparisons using "like" or "as" (e.g., She was as brave as a lion).

Personification: Giving human qualities to non-human things (e.g., The flowers danced in the breeze).

Alliteration: Repetition of the same sound at the beginning of adjacent words (e.g., Sally sells seashells by the seashore).

Onomatopoeia: Words that imitate the sound they represent (e.g., The thunder rumbled).

Explain (10 minutes): Discuss why authors use figurative language in their writing. Explain that it helps readers create mental images and adds depth to the text.

Elaborate (5 minutes): Ask students to brainstorm why they think using figurative language can be important in creative writing. Encourage them to think about how it can enhance their stories and descriptions.

Practicing Figurative Language

Engage (10 minutes): Start by reviewing the types of figurative language from the previous day's lesson. Ask a few students to give examples of each.

Explore (15 minutes): Distribute handouts with examples of similes, personification, alliteration, and onomatopoeia. Have students work in pairs or small groups to identify and discuss the examples.

Explain (10 minutes): Lead a class discussion on the handout, going through each example and discussing its effectiveness in creating imagery or mood in writing.

Elaborate (10 minutes): Provide students with creative writing prompts or worksheets that require them to incorporate similes, personification, alliteration, and onomatopoeia into short paragraphs or poems. Encourage them to be creative and use their imaginations.

Evaluate (15 minutes): Ask students to share their writing with the class, focusing on how they incorporated figurative language. Provide constructive feedback and discuss the impact of figurative language on the writing.

Conclusion (5 minutes): Summarize the importance of using similes, personification, alliteration, and onomatopoeia in creative writing.

Encourage students to continue practicing and exploring figurative language in their writing to make it more engaging and vivid.

Induction Activities

Introduction to Figurative Language

Induction Activity (15 minutes): Start with a figurative language scavenger hunt. Give students a short passage from a book or poem that contains examples of similes, personification, alliteration, and onomatopoeia. Have them work in pairs or small groups to identify and underline or highlight these examples. Afterward, discuss their findings as a class.

Sample Passages:

1. "The wind howled like a hungry wolf outside the window, and the rain tapped on the roof like a thousand tiny drummers. Inside, the old house creaked and groaned, as if it had a life of its own. The trees outside whispered secrets to each other, and the leaves danced in the moonlight. It was a night full of magic."

2. "The sun peeked over the horizon, spreading its golden fingers across the sky. Birds greeted the day with cheerful songs, and the flowers in the garden nodded their heads in agreement. The river chuckled as it flowed lazily by, and the trees whispered ancient stories to anyone who would listen."

Practising Figurative Language

Induction Activity (10 minutes):

Begin with a "Figurative Language Showcase."

Prepare a display of visual aids or posters that depict various figurative language examples, such as images of roaring thunder (onomatopoeia), a talking sun (personification), a snake slithering silently (alliteration), and a river babbling (personification).

Ask students to silently observe these visuals and jot down what they notice or feel about each one. Afterward, have a brief class discussion about their observations, emphasizing the impact of figurative language in creating mental images and mood.

Including these induction activities will help engage students and make the lessons more interactive and enjoyable.

Induction activity for similes using any song.

You can use a popular song to introduce the concept of similes to your students.

Induction Activity for Similes: Song Analysis

Materials:

- A projector or screen for displaying lyrics (if available).
- Printed lyrics of a song with prominent similes. You can choose a song like "Firework" by Katy Perry, "Brave" by Sara Bareilles, or "Imagine" by John Lennon, "Everything at all at once" by Lenka which contain similes in their lyrics.
- Whiteboard and markers or a chalkboard and chalk.
- Writing materials for students.

Procedure:

Introduction (5 minutes): Begin by explaining to the students what similes are. You can say, "Similes are comparisons between two different things using the words 'like' or 'as.' They help us create vivid mental images in our minds. Today, we'll explore similes through a song."

Listening Activity (10 minutes): Play the chosen song (make sure to use clean and appropriate lyrics). As students listen, ask them to pay attention to any phrases that use "like" or "as" to compare two things. You can provide copies of the printed lyrics if available or display them on a screen.

Group Discussion (5 minutes): After listening to the song, have students work in small groups to identify and discuss the similes they heard in the lyrics. Encourage them to write down at least three similes from the song.

Class Discussion (5 minutes): Bring the class back together and ask each group to share one simile they found. Write these similes on the board or chalkboard.

Analysis (5 minutes): Discuss with the class how the similes from the song helped create vivid mental images and emotions. Ask students how they felt when they heard these similes in the song. This discussion will help them understand the purpose and impact of similes in writing.

Application (5 minutes): Provide each student with a blank sheet of paper and ask them to come up with a simile of their own. Encourage creativity and ask them to share their similes with the class.

Conclusion (5 minutes): Summarize the lesson by emphasizing the importance of similes in adding depth and imagery to writing. Encourage students to look for similes in the books they read and in their daily lives.

Here's a bank of 30 similes that you can use for various writing exercises or to help students understand and incorporate similes in their writing:

> As brave as a lion.
> As busy as a bee.
> As sly as a fox.
> As swift as a cheetah.
> As light as a feather.
> As bright as the sun.
> As cold as ice.
> As clear as crystal.
> As quick as lightning.
> As gentle as a lamb.
> As wise as an owl.

> ➢ As busy as a beaver.
> ➢ As stubborn as a mule.
> ➢ As quiet as a mouse.
> ➢ As busy as an ant.
> ➢ As graceful as a swan.
> ➢ As strong as an ox.
> ➢ As slippery as an eel.
> ➢ As soft as velvet.
> ➢ As fresh as a daisy.
> ➢ As busy as a squirrel.
> ➢ As hungry as a wolf.
> ➢ As smooth as silk.
> ➢ As fierce as a tiger.
> ➢ As shiny as a diamond.
> ➢ As slow as molasses.
> ➢ As deep as the ocean.
> ➢ As playful as a kitten.
> ➢ As happy as a clam.
> ➢ As free as a bird.

These similes can be used to enrich descriptions, create imagery, and add depth to writing. Encourage students to use them to make their writing more engaging and vivid.

Induction activity for onomatopoeia

An engaging way to introduce the concept of onomatopoeia to students is through a hands-on sound activity. Here's an induction activity for onomatopoeia:

Induction Activity for Onomatopoeia: Sound Exploration

Materials:

> ➢ A variety of objects that can produce distinct sounds (e.g., a bell, a rubber ball, a squeaky toy, a tambourine, a whistle, a crumpled piece of paper).

- ➢ Blindfolds (optional).
- ➢ Whiteboard and markers or a chalkboard and chalk.
- ➢ Writing materials for students.

Introduction: Start by explaining to students that you will be exploring a fun and unique aspect of language called "onomatopoeia." Explain that onomatopoeia are words that imitate or represent sounds.

Object Sounds: Place the variety of objects that make distinct sounds on a table at the front of the classroom. Invite individual students to come to the front and choose an object. Ask them to make the sound of the chosen object for the class. For example, if they choose a bell, they should ring it. If they choose a squeaky toy, they should squeeze it. If you want to add an element of surprise and suspense, you can blindfold the students before they choose the object.

Class Discussion: After each student makes a sound, discuss with the class how the sound relates to onomatopoeia. Ask students if the sound they heard reminded them of any words. Write down any onomatopoeic words that arise on the whiteboard or chalkboard.

Brainstorming: As a class, brainstorm more onomatopoeic words together. Encourage students to think about sounds they hear in their daily lives, such as the sound of rain, a dog barking, or a car honking. List these words on the board as well.

Application: Ask each student to choose one onomatopoeic word from the list or come up with their own. Have them write a sentence or short phrase that includes this word. For example, if they choose "buzz," they could write, "The bees buzzed around the garden."

Conclusion: Summarize the activity by reinforcing the concept of onomatopoeia. Explain that these words help create vivid and sensory-rich writing, allowing readers to hear the sounds in their minds as they read. Encourage students to be on the lookout for onomatopoeic words in literature and to use them in their writing.

This hands-on sound exploration activity will not only introduce onomatopoeia but also make it a memorable and engaging concept for students.

Induction activity for personification

Induction Activity for Personification: "Give an Object a Voice"

Materials:

> ➤ A variety of everyday objects (e.g., a pencil, a chair, a lamp, a shoe, a book).
> ➤ Whiteboard and markers or a chalkboard and chalk.
> ➤ Writing materials for students.

Procedure:

Introduction: Begin by explaining to students that they will be exploring a literary device called "personification." Personification is when human qualities or characteristics are given to non-human things or objects. It helps make writing more vivid and engaging.

Object Selection: Display the variety of everyday objects you've gathered at the front of the classroom. Ask each student to choose one object that they will personify in their writing.

Object's Personality: Instruct students to think about what kind of personality or characteristics they want to give to their chosen object. For example, a pencil might become talkative and eager to write, while a lamp might become wise and calming. Have students jot down a few notes about their chosen object's personality.

Writing Activity: Ask students to write a short paragraph or dialogue in which their chosen object comes to life and speaks or interacts with them. Encourage them to use descriptive language to convey the object's personality. For example, a talking pencil might say, "I can't wait to create beautiful stories with you," while a wise lamp might offer advice like, "In the darkest times, I'll always be here to light your way."

Sharing and Discussion: Invite a few students to share their written pieces with the class. As they share, discuss how they personified their objects and how it added depth and interest to their writing.

Class Brainstorm: Ask the class to brainstorm other objects they could personify and what unique personalities those objects might have. Write down a list of objects and their potential personalities on the whiteboard or chalkboard.

Conclusion: Summarize the activity by emphasizing the power of personification in making writing more creative and relatable. Encourage students to use personification in their future creative writing to bring their stories and characters to life.

This activity allows students to explore personification in a fun and imaginative way, making it easier for them to grasp the concept and apply it in their writing.

<u>Sample:</u>

1. Object: Water Bottle

Personification: The water bottle sat on the table, its plastic body glistening with condensation. It looked eager, waiting to quench someone's thirst. As I reached for it, it seemed to sigh with relief, knowing its purpose was about to be fulfilled. "Ah, there you are," it seemed to say, "I've been patiently holding this refreshing drink just for you. Let's stay hydrated together."

2. Object: Alarm Clock

Personification: The alarm clock perched on the bedside table, its digital numbers flashing in the dim morning light. It appeared impatient, as if it couldn't wait to do its duty. When the appointed hour arrived, it let out a loud and insistent beep, like an eager friend waking you up for an adventure. "Rise and shine," it announced cheerfully, "a new day awaits, and I'm here to greet it with you!"

Here's a list of 20 objects that you can use for personification exercises or writing prompts:

- Mirror
- Camera
- Umbrella
- Bicycle
- Guitar
- Coffee Mug
- Flashlight
- Window
- Backpack
- Sneakers
- Candle
- Paintbrush
- Globe
- Pocket Watch
- Sunglasses
- Sunflower
- Piano
- Compass
- Map
- Laptop

Feel free to use these objects for personification exercises or creative writing prompts to encourage students to think creatively and vividly in their writing.

4.3 Sample Worksheets:

1. Find the onomatopoeia in each sentence and underline it:

1. My sister can burp the alphabet.
2. The tree has been buzzing with insects since it bloomed.
3. When she opened the cash register, it went, "ca-ching!"
4. The birds in the bush outside of my window are chirping.
5. Her heels clacked across the tile floor.

2. Fill in the blanks with the correct sound word:

1. When a cow is hungry, she goes ______________.
2. The dropped egg went ______________.
3. The girl went ______________ on the drum.
4. ______________ went the coins as they dropped into the piggy bank.
5. When I jump into the swimming pool, the water goes __________.
6. A police car went ______________ as it passed the busy street.
7. The bed went ______________ as I bounced on it.
8. Mrs June's bell made a ______________ sound.
9. ______________ went Sanjeep's drink as he reached the bottom of the cup.
10. The balloon went ______________ as the children stood on it.

3. Read each sentence carefully, then choose an example of onomatopoeia from the word box to complete the sentence:

chatter	gurgled	screech	howled	neighed	growled
rustled	flutter	sizzling	clanged	howling	gushed

1. The horse _____________ at the sight of its owner.
2. The dog _____________ menacingly at the strangers.
3. The river _____________ as it passed over the rocky mountain terrain.
4. The Monarch butterflies _____________ as they take flight.
5. At night the wind was _____________ in the darkness.
6. The bells of the church _____________ to announce the start of the service.
7. The mountain wolf _____________ at the full moon.
8. The sports car swerved to a halt with a loud _____________ .
9. The flood water _____________ into the surrounding fields causing chaos and destruction.
10. The bacon _____________ in the frying pan could be heard from the kitchen.
11. The leaves _____________ gently in the cool Autumn breeze.
12. The _____________ from the pupils dissipated as the principal entered the assembly hall.

4. Rewrite each sentence using a simile:

1. The girl is beautiful.

____

____

2. I am busy.

____

____

3. My mother is very calm.

____

____

4. The butterfly is colourful.

____

____

5. My bottle is blue.

____

____

5. Alliteration repeats the first letter or sound of a word. Circle the examples of alliteration below:

1. Abigail absentmindedly altered the albatross artwork.
2. His heart was beating like a big brass band.
3. Children who treat their things badly will lose their toys.
4. When Wednesday comes, will you walk with me?
5. I absolutely cannot stand that.
6. Mushrooms grow membranes in mostly moist and dark places.
7. The goat was chewing on the leaves.
8. Jack jumped over a jaguar and Jill joined in.

6. Fill in the Blanks: Add a word to these sentences that works with the alliteration.

1. My mum makes me munch ______________ on a Monday morning.
2. The reigning royal was ______________ about the rain.
3. Fancy foxes fly over ______________.
4. ______________ cooked in the crockpot are crazy good.
5. Elephants eat enormous ______________ every day.

7. Repetition is when a word or phrase is repeated within a sentence or text. Circle the sentences that contain repetition below. Not every example has repetition, it is your job to identify which ones do.

1. What about breakfast? What about lunch? What about dinner? What about pudding?
2. A horse is a horse, of course, he's a horse.
3. Arthur absolutely adored apples.
4. O Captain, my Captain!
5. I saw the sun one sweet summer day.
6. Hark how the bells, sweet silver bells, all seem to say throw cares away.
7. Once upon a time, a king lived in a castle.
8. Never give in - never, never, never.

8. Circle or underline the phrase that is repeated in these examples:

1. Let it snow, let it snow, let it snow.
2. To be or not to be?
3. If you can dream - and not make dreams your master, if you can think – and not make thoughts your aim...
4. Yes, I will swim across the ocean. Yes, I will walk across the desert. Yes, I will see you again.
5. I will try again when I fall down, I will try again when things are hard, I will try again when I fail.

Sample Literature References:

1) Onomatopoeia:

"Some fish are a noisy lot. Hawaiian trigger fish <u>grind</u> their teeth loudly, the male toadfish <u>growls</u>, bottlenose dolphins <u>click</u> and <u>squeal</u> like badly oiled office chairs: bowhead whales <u>purr</u> and <u>twerp</u>; humpback whales put on a <u>songfest</u>."-A Natural History of the Senses, by Diane Ackerman

2) Personification:

"Five-fingered ferns hung over the water and dropped spray from their fingertips." – Flight, by John Steinbeck

3) Simile:

"He looks like right after the maul hits the steer and it no longer alive and don't yet know that it is dead." — As I Lay Dying, by William Faulkner

"O my Love is like a red, red rose That's newly sprung in June; O my Love is like the melody That's sweetly played in tune." — A Red, Red Rose by Robert Burns

"The cafe was like a battleship stripped for action" — The Sun Also Rises by Ernest Hemingway

IMAGERY

5.1 Introduction:

Imagery is language used by poets, novelists and other writers to create images in the mind of the reader. It uses our Five senses of what we see, hear, smell, taste and feel.

@prineelenglishacademy

Visual Imagery

Visual imagery describes what we see: comic book images, paintings, or images directly experienced through the narrator's eyes. Visual imagery may include:

Color, such as: burnt red, bright orange, dull yellow, verdant green, and Robin's egg blue.

Shapes, such as: square, circular, tubular, rectangular, and conical.

Size, such as: miniscule, tiny, small, medium-sized, large, and gigantic.

Pattern, such as: polka-dotted, striped, zig-zagged, jagged, and straight.

Auditory Imagery

Auditory imagery describes what we hear, from music to noise to pure silence. Auditory imagery may include:

Enjoyable sounds, such as: beautiful music, birdsong, and the voices of a chorus.

Noises, such as: the bang of a gun, the sound of a broom moving across the floor, and the sound of broken glass shattering on the hard floor.

The lack of noise, describing a peaceful calm or eerie silence., well

Tactile Imagery

Tactile imagery describes what we feel or touch. Tactile imagery includes:

Temperature, such as bitter cold, humidity, mildness, and stifling heat.

Texture, such as rough, ragged, seamless, and smooth.

Touch, such as hand-holding, one's in the grass, or the feeling of starched fabric on one's skin.

Movement, such as burning muscles from exertion, swimming in cold water, or kicking a soccer ball.

Olfactory Imagery

Olfactory imagery describes what we smell. Olfactory imagery may include:

Fragrances, such as perfumes, enticing food and drink, and blooming flowers.

Odours, such as rotting trash, body odors, or a stinky wet dog.

Gustatory Imagery

Gustatory imagery describes what we taste. Gustatory imagery can include:

Sweetness, such as candies, cookies, and desserts.

Sourness, bitterness, and tartness, such as lemons and limes.

Saltiness, such as pretzels, French fries, and pepperonis.

Spiciness, such as salsas and curries.

Savoriness, such as thick soup.

5.2 vocabulary Bank

VOCABULARY TO DESCRIBE COLOUR

The use of uncommon colour names, when used as adjectives, creates wonderful **visual imagery** that makes your reader see **specific colours** and shades in the objects you are trying to describe. This lifts the quality of your writing effortlessly and gives it beauty and sophistication.

Intensity

Brilliant	Clear	Dark
Glassy	Iridescent	Light

Red

Burgundy	Cherry
Crimson	Scarlet

Blue

Azure	Celeste	Cobalt
Cadet	Cerulean	Cornflower

Green

Apple	Aquamarine	Asparagus
Aqua	Army	Celadon

Yellow

Citreous	Mustard
Golden	Primrose
Honey	Topaz

Black

Ebony	Licorice	Pitch
Jet	Morel	Sable

Brown

Auburn	Brass	Burnt sienna
Bole	Burnet	Castor

Purple

Eggplant	Indigo	Puce
Brinjal	Lilac	Thistle

Grey

Blue-green	Dapple	Dove grey
Blue-grey	Dish-water	Steel

Pink

Plum	Coral	Ibis
Peach	Deep pink	Hot pink

White

Alice	Marble	Snow
Chalk	Milk	

Off white

Buff	Cornsilk	Linen
Almond	Cream	Off white

Orange

Amber	Saffron	Apricot
Carrot	Burnt orange	Orange-red

VOCABULARY TO DESCRIBE SOUND

Poets and writers use sounds to **energise** their writing and make it a more **vivid experience** for the reader. Sounds can be **hard** or **soft** to create **mood** and **atmosphere** in writing. Sound words are called **onomatopoeias**.

Sounds can be used metaphorically to convey more than just sound. They can be made to convey feeling, connotation and extra meaning through comparisons.

Sound

Ahem	Beep	Blast	Blabber	Buzz
Chirp	Cackle	Chatter	Clash	Cough
Explode	Flutter	Gasp	Giggle	Gaggle
Hiss	Howl	Laugh	Mumble	Moan
Shush	Shriek	Screech	Snore	Thud
Whimper	Whisper	Whistle	Whine	Zoom

Simple onomatopoeia: The sheep <u>bleated</u> when the wolf came forward.

Metaphoric use: He <u>bleated</u> for mercy but the king did not stir.

VOCABULARY TO DESCRIBE SMELL

Use words of smell to create **accurate feelings** in the readers. A lot of writers use similes and analogies of various other objects to describe smells.

Smell words

Acid	Fragrant	Musty	Spicy
Acrid	Fresh	Odorous	Spoiled
Aromatic	Fresh	Perfumed	Stale
Balmy	Fruity	Piney	Sickly-Sweet
Bouquet	Gaseous	Plastic	Stagnant
Briny	Heady	Pungent	Stench
Burnt	Incense	Putrid	Stink
Damp	Lemony	Putrid	Stuffy
Dank	Lime	Rancid	Sty
Dirty	Loamy	Reeking	Nauseating
Doggy	Melancholy	Rotten	Sweaty
Earthy	Mildewed	Savoury	Sweet
Embarrassing	Minty	Scented	Fang

Fetid	Moist	Sharp	Tart
Fishy	Morbid	Sickly	Unpleasant
Flowery	Mouldy	Sour	Whiff

VOCABULARY TO DESCRIBE TASTE

Taste is our primary sense through which we know the world around us. Taste words are generally described through the known tastes of foods we eat. Smell and taste work together to produce flavours.

Taste Words

Acerbic	Distasteful	Mild	Scrumptious
Acidic	Divine	Minty	Sharp
Acrid	Dry	Moist	Sickening
Alkaline	Enjoyable	Mouth Watering	Sour
Alluring	Enticing	Nauseating	Smelly
Appealing	Fetid	Nutty	Spicy
Appetizing	Fiery	Oily	Spoiled
Astringent	Fishy	Overripe	Stale
Barbed	Flat	Palatable	Stinging
Bitter	Flavourful	Peppery	Succulent
Bittersweet	Foul	Piercing	Sugary
Biting	Fruity	Piquant	Sweet
Bland	Gelatinous	Pointed	Tangy
Brackish	Gingery	Potent	Tantalizing
Briny	Greasy	Prickly	Tart
Burnt	Hearty	Pungent	Tasteless
Buttery	Heavenly	Rancid	Tasty
Candied	Honeyed	Rank	Tempting
Caustic	Hot	Raw	Trenchant
Celestial	Insipid	Repulsive	Unappetising

Cheesy	Inviting	Revolting	Unpleasant
Choking	Juicy	Rich	Unripe
Crisp	Lemony	Ripe	Vinegary
Cutting	Luscious	Robust	Vitriolic
Delectable	Lip Smacking	Rotten	Voluptuous
Delicious	Malodorous	Salty	Zesty
Delightful	Medicinal	Satisfying	Zing
Disgusting	Mellow	Savoury	

Food

Abundant	Delicacy	Mash	Season
Aftertaste	Desire	Marinated	Sizzle
Appetite	Drizzle	Over	Spices
Baste	Epicurean	Passion	Spread
Blistering	Garnish	Pickled	Sprout
Boiling	Gastronomical	Preserved	Squeeze
Burning	Gourmand	Ravenous	Starchy
Condiments	Gourmet	Relish	Stuff
Cooking	Ground	Savour	Sumptuous
Craving	Herbs	Scanty	Whipped
Crust	Lavish	Scorch	

Action Words

Approach	Cudgel	Crawl	Ascend
Assemble	Dance	Cripple	Clench
Capture	Depart	Dangle	Crush
Cascade	Chase	Dawdle	Destroy
Clasp	Clamber	Descend	Gag
Climb	Cling	Burst	Gallop
Crash	Clutch	Crouch	Hasten

Crept	Construct	Descend	Mount
Play	Rush	Spin	Swap
Plummet	Scavenge	Sprint	Sweep
Hurry	Select	Stitch	Press
Move	Skip	Quake	Propel
Plunder	Slap	Quench	Punch
Pluck	Slide	Remove	Quarrel
Plunge	Slither	Return	Quiver
Pounce	Slump	Stomp	Reduce
Smother	Sneak	Suffocate	Reverberate
Run	Turn	Tremble	Withdraw
Shiver	Twist	Tumble	Wrestle
Shrink	Thrust	Twirl	Swipe
Slaughter	Trample	Wobble	Thunder
Slouch	Waggle	Wriggle	Split
Splash	Wipe	Zoom	
Stumble	Swarm	Swirl	

VOCABULARY TO DESCRIBE SLOW MOVEMENT

Slow Movement words needs to be employed to show emotional impact on characters, trauma, shock, age, listlessness, stealth and caution in actions.

Words For Slow Movement

Amble	Droop	Saunter	Stray
Bend	Edge	Slink	Stroll
Crawl	Heave	Slouch	Swagger
Creep	Loiter	Sneak	Sway
Drag	Lumber	Stagger	Tiptoe
Drift	Plod	Stalk	Waddle

Words For Fast Movement

Bolt	Hope	Sail	Sprint
Bounce	Hurl	Scamper	Streak
Careen	Hurry	Scramble	Stride
Chase	Lift	Scurry	Swat
Dart	Odorous	Shove	Swerve
Dash	Plummet	Skip	Swing
Drive	Plunge	Smash	Swoop
Drop	Propel	Soar	Trot
Flee	Race	Speed	Whisk
Flick	Ram	Spin	Zip
Fly	Run	Spring	Zoom
Gallop	Rush		

5.3 Lesson Plan:

Lesson plan for imagery for secondary grades

Objective: Students will be able to use descriptive language to create mental images for the reader through the use of imagery.

Materials:

- ➤ Examples of descriptive imagery from literature or online sources
- ➤ Pencils and paper
- ➤ A variety of objects, pictures, or scenes for students to describe

Introduction:

Start by asking students if they have ever read a book that painted a vivid picture in their minds. Explain that authors use descriptive language to create mental images for the reader. Introduce the concept of imagery and explain that it is a type of language that appeals to the senses and creates a picture in the reader's mind.

Development:

- Read examples of descriptive imagery from literature or online sources, and discuss the images created. Ask students which senses were appealed to in each example.
- Provide a variety of objects, pictures, or scenes for students to describe using imagery. Encourage them to use descriptive words that appeal to the senses and create a mental image for the reader.
- After students have had some practice, have them work in pairs or small groups to create a short descriptive paragraph using imagery. Encourage them to share their paragraphs with the class.

Closure: As a closing activity, have students share their descriptive paragraphs with the class. Encourage the class to visualize the images being described and ask them which senses were appealed to in each paragraph.

Assessment: Assess students' understanding of imagery by reviewing their descriptive paragraphs and identifying the use of descriptive language that appeals to the senses. Provide feedback to help them improve their use of imagery.

Imagery lesson plan for primary grades.

Objective: Students will be able to use descriptive language to create mental images for the reader through the use of imagery.

- ➢ Materials:
- ➢ Examples of descriptive imagery from children's literature or online sources
- ➢ Pencils and paper
- ➢ A variety of objects, pictures, or scenes for students to describe

Introduction:

- Show kids a picture of a beach, park or a Mall.

- Discuss with them what they see, hear, sell, taste and feel at those places. List them out in various columns.
- Give them an organiser to note down various ideas.
- Read examples of descriptive imagery from children's literature and discuss the images created. Ask students which senses were appealed to in each example.
- Provide a variety of objects, pictures, or scenes for students to describe using imagery. Encourage them to use descriptive words that appeal to the senses and create a mental image for the reader.
- After students have had some practice, have them work in pairs or small groups to create a short descriptive paragraph using imagery. Encourage them to share their paragraphs with the class.

Closure: As a closing activity, have students share their descriptive paragraphs with the class. Encourage the class to visualize the images being described and ask them which senses were appealed to in each paragraph.

Assessment: Assess students' understanding of imagery by reviewing their descriptive paragraphs and identifying the use of descriptive language that appeals to the senses. Provide feedback to help them improve their use of imagery.

Extension: For an extension activity, have students create imagery of their bedroom, kitchen or any other interesting place they might visit.

Sample Imagery/descriptive paragraphs:

Use of Imagery in Sentences

- ➤ Iwan's sweaty gym clothes left a stale odour in the locker room; so, they had to keep the windows open.
- ➤ The tasty, salty broth soothed her sore throat as Simran ate the warm soup.
- ➤ Glittering white, the blanket of snow-covered everything in sight and also blocked the street.

> ➢ The tree bark was rough against the deer's skin but it did satisfy its itch.
> ➢ Kids could hear the popping and crackling as their mom dropped the bacon into the frying pan, and soon the salty, greasy smell wafted toward me.

Examples from Literature:

1. Ruskin Bond, the renowned Indian author, is also known for his descriptive and vivid imagery. Here's an example of his imagery from his book "The Blue Umbrella":

"The hills were draped in a misty veil, and the valleys below were filled with a soft, hazy light. The rain had stopped, but the air was still heavy with the scent of wet earth and greenery. Drops of water clung to the leaves, and the sound of trickling water could be heard from the streams and rivulets that flowed down the slopes. The whole scene was one of tranquillity and beauty, a world washed clean by the rain."

2. Here's another example of Ruskin Bond's imagery, from his book "The Room on the Roof":

"The trees were in full bloom, their branches heavy with pink and white blossoms that seemed to glow in the sunlight. The air was filled with the sweet fragrance of flowers, and the sound of bees buzzing as they flitted from one blossom to the next. In the distance, the hills rose up, their jagged peaks piercing the clear blue sky. It was a scene of breath-taking beauty, one that made Rusty feel as if he were a part of something larger than himself."

3. Here's another example of imagery from J.K. Rowling's "Harry Potter and the Half-Blood Prince":

"The fog was lowering, and Harry, Ron, and Hermione could hardly see where they were going. As they walked along the edge of the lake, their footsteps echoed through the stillness, and the water lapped gently at the bank. Suddenly, Harry saw something glimmering in the distance - a light. They hurried towards it, and as they got closer, they saw that it was coming from the windows of Hagrid's hut, which was perched on the edge of the Forbidden Forest."

4. Here's an example of imagery from Enid Blyton's "The Enchanted Wood", which is part of the Faraway Tree series:

"The trees were so tall that they seemed to touch the sky, and their branches were thick with leaves and blossom. The leaves rustled in the breeze, and the flowers filled the air with a sweet fragrance. Every now and then, a bird would fly out from the branches, chirping a merry tune. It was a magical place, filled with wonder and excitement, and the children couldn't wait to explore it."

5. Here's another example of imagery from Enid Blyton's "The Magic Faraway Tree":

"Their eyes grew big with wonder as they looked up at the enormous tree above them. Its trunk was wide enough for five children to stand with arms outstretched, and it disappeared into the clouds. The branches were thick with leaves, and on them grew strange and beautiful fruits that the children had never seen before. The air was filled with the sound of rustling leaves and the chirping of birds, and the scent of flowers and fruit wafted up to them on the gentle breeze."

6. Here's another example of imagery from L.M. Montgomery's "Anne of Green Gables":

"The sun was setting when they drove into the yard at Green Gables. The western sky was a great arc of crystal, smitten here and there with opal hues, and flushing with prismatized lights. Over the long green field of the house a mirage floated – a mirage of firelit dew. It might have been fairyland. 'Could you imagine anything more beautiful than the things we saw?' said Anne, stopping for breath.

- **How imagery can be used to describe the setting of a place:**

"The library was a sanctuary of knowledge and imagination, a place where books of every size and shape lined the shelves like sentinels. The air was still and quiet, broken only by the soft rustling of pages and the occasional whisper of a patron seeking assistance. The smell of leather-bound tomes and old paper mingled with the faint scent of coffee from the small café tucked into a corner of the room. Sunlight filtered through stained-glass windows, casting rainbow patterns on the carpeted floor. Each corner of the room held a secret waiting to be discovered, and each book was a key to unlock a new world of wonder."

"The airport was a bustling hub of activity, filled with the sounds of excited chatter, clattering luggage carts, and the roar of airplanes taking off and landing. The air was alive with the scent of jet fuel and the sweet aroma of baked goods from the nearby cafes. Long rows of seats lined the walkways, their metal frames glinting in the bright lights that illuminated the cavernous space. People of all ages and nationalities rushed by, their faces alight with anticipation and excitement for their upcoming journeys. The vast expanse of windows offered a panoramic view of the tarmac, where planes of every shape and size waited to whisk their passengers away to destinations unknown."

5.3 Sample Worksheets:

Q. Look at the pictures and record all the words you can think of that relate to these senses. Then write a paragraph on those pictures using the points:

1.

2.

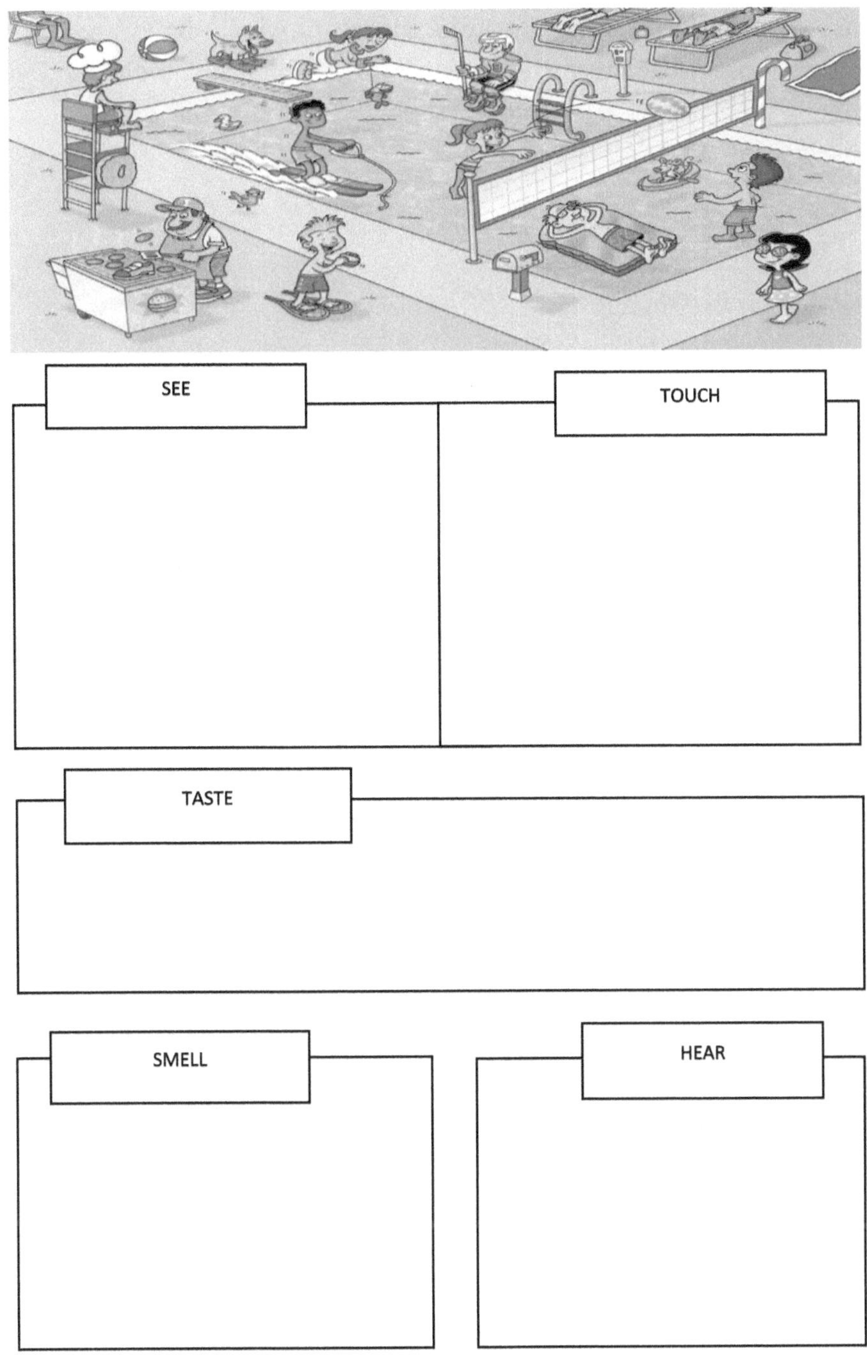

<table>
<tr><td>SEE</td><td>TOUCH</td></tr>
</table>

TASTE

SMELL

HEAR

5.4 Question Bank:

Read the situations, settings, and places provided below. Use your imagination and creativity to create a vivid image of each one using Imagery and figurative language.

1. A beach at sunset
2. A crowded city street
3. A deserted island
4. A forest in the fall
5. A mountain range in winter
6. A school cafeteria during lunchtime
7. A carnival at night
8. A spaceship traveling through space
9. A rainy day in the city
10. A library on a quiet afternoon

CHAPTER 6

SHOW, DON'T TELL

6.1 Introduction:

What is Show don't tell?

The writer, Anton Chekhov, defined *Show don't tell* like this:

Don't tell me the moon is shining; show me the glint of light on the broken glass.

The difference between Show and Tell

As a writer, your goal is to provoke a reaction in your readers, take them to feel the emotions your character is feeling.

The difference between show and tell is that show invokes on the reader a mental image of the scene/emotion, while tell is a statement of an action/emotion.

Show

Show is a tool used to pull the reader to a scene. By using it, you're creating a connection between the reader and your scene/character.

Showing concrete and vivid details will make the reader create his own conclusions — that will be the same as yours, only he's going to interpret them by himself.

Show keeps the readers actively involved in the story. *Tell* will keep them passive on the plot.

Readers don't want to be told the character is angry, sad, or happy. They want to feel it!

When the writer shows the story from the character's perspective, hardly the readers will drop the book — they're living *with* the character, the events are them as well. The readers see, listen, think and feel what the character lives.

6.2 Strategies to implement Show don't Tell in your writing:

1. Use the character's five senses (Refer Imagery)

Take the reader to the scene through the character's senses.

Make a list of what the character sees, listen, feels, touch or taste. Then rewrite the scene using strong verbs.

2. Use strong verbs

Strong verbs are the irregular ones, they are dynamic and, often, have a connotation of movement, they create a vivid image in the reader's mind.

Strong verbs are action words that are more descriptive and powerful than their weaker counterparts. They add more meaning and detail to a sentence, and often help to paint a

clearer picture of the action being described.

For example, instead of using a weak verb like "walked," a strong verb like "sauntered" or "strode" could be used to convey a more specific and vivid image of the action. Similarly, instead of using a weak verb like "said," a strong verb like "exclaimed" or "murmured" could be used to add more emotion and nuance to the dialogue.

Strong verbs can help to make writing more interesting and engaging for the reader, as they create a more vivid and descriptive image of the action being described.

But this is not a rule to be always used. Weak verbs are part of the writing, and they have value. However, when writing crucial scenes, if you want to create tension or to highlight a scene, use strong verbs.

3. Avoid adverbs

Adverbs distract the reader of the story, they put you, the writer, on the scene. It's you who's giving meaning to an action. Moreover, in the story, there's only place for the characters and the reader (you don't belong there).

Take this as an example: "Richard walked, *slowly*, through the avenue."

Including the adverb, I've interfered with your reading. Instead, I could have shown, like this:

"Richard walked on the avenue, he stopped to smell the flowers, he admired the blue sky, smiled at the squirrels, running up the trees."

If Richard were in a hurry, he wouldn't stop to smell the flowers or look at the sky. Being descriptive, *I've shown* how Richard was calm and walking slowly.

Besides, I've also shown that Richard is a person sensitive to nature. If I wanted to let you know that he was angry, I would show him nagging about the children's noise.

Showing a scene, we are also allowing the reader to build a profile of the character. By himself, without our interference.

When using adverbs (which is not wrong, they must be used only if they give real meaning to the sentence).

5. Use dialogue

Dialogue is the easiest way of *showing*. It's action in real-time; life occurring in that exact moment. A dialogue is always *show*.

Here's an example of how to use dialogue to show, rather than tell:

1. Telling: Samantha was angry at her friend for cancelling their plans.

Showing: "What the hell, Kate? We made plans for weeks and you cancel on me at the last minute?" Samantha said, clenching her fists.

2. Telling: John was nervous about his job interview.

Showing: "Okay John, take a deep breath and just be yourself," said his roommate, patting him on the back.

"I don't know, man. What if I mess up? What if I don't get the job?" John replied, fidgeting with his tie.

In this example, we use dialogue to show John's nervousness and anxiety about his upcoming job interview. By including his dialogue and physical action of fidgeting with his tie, we get a better sense of how John is feeling and can empathize with his situation.

3. Telling: Emily was happy to see her best friend after a long time.

Showing: As soon as she saw her friend's face, Emily let out a high-pitched scream and ran towards her, arms wide open. "Oh my god, it's so good to see you!" she exclaimed, hugging her tightly.

6. Focus on actions and reactions (Face, Body and Voice)

Don't tell the traits of the personality of your characters: show them through their actions. Allow the reader to see how the character acts and reacts to the events in the plot. That will reveal his personality.

Instead of saying, "she's a bad woman" describe her kicking a straight dog. You will, immediately, convince the reader she's not a good person.

here are a few examples of how to use show, not tell to depict character traits:

1. Compassionate:

Telling: Sarah was a compassionate person.

Showing: Sarah stopped to help an elderly woman struggling with her groceries, carrying them all the way to her doorstep.

2. Brave:

Telling: Jake was a brave soldier.

Showing: Jake charged into the battlefield, despite the sounds of gunfire and screams of pain around him. He pulled his wounded comrade to safety and continued fighting.

3. Stubborn:

Telling: Emily was a stubborn person.

Showing: Emily refused to give up on her dream of becoming a professional singer, despite numerous rejections and setbacks. She continued to practice every day and eventually landed her first gig.

Besides, focus on body language and facial expressions: they are part of how we communicate. When we talk, we react, physically. So, the characters should also have that.

Conclusion

With practice, *show don't tell* will become easier, to a point, whereas it'll be spontaneous in your writing.

In short: showing illustrates, while telling merely states.

How do you show not tell the character's feelings and emotions?

Say, we want to show character's happiness.

1. Sadia is happy.

We show how the character's face looks, body moves and what character's says (how their voice sounds)

F- grinning from ear to ear, eyes twinkling, blushing cheeks etc.

B- jumping with joy, dancing and twirling etc.

V- squealing with excitement, singing, shouting with excitement etc.

2. Sophie is angry.

We show how the character's face looks, body moves and what We show what the character's says (how their voice sounds)

F- eyes blood red, pursed lips, face red, narrowed eyebrows etc.

B- clenched fists, punched fists, body shaking, veins popping, hands on hips etc.

V- yelling, erupting like volcano, etc.

6.3 BANK for EMOTIONS

EMOTIONS & FEELINGS

Afraid	Nervous
Hands Shaking	Tapping Hands Or Feet
Knees Like Jelly	Bitting Bottom Lip/Nails
Covered Mouth With Hand	Bufferflies In Stomach
Heavy, Fast Breathing	Lump In Your Throat
Heart Pounding	Playing With Hair
Whimpering	Stuttering

Embarrased	Angry
Blushing/Turn Red	Red In The Face
Hanging Head Low	Hands On Hips
Holding Back Tears	Jaw/Fists Clenched
Rolling Eyes	Veins Popping
Stomatch Tightens	Dark Squinted Eyes
Hiding Face	Punching Fist Into The Air

Hot	Happpy
Bright Red Face	Smiling Face
Sweat On Face/Back	Eyes Wide Open
Fanning Self With Hand	Corners Of Mouth Rising
Moving Slowly	Jumping Up And Down

Panting For Breath	Laughing
Drenched Hairline	Giggling
	On 'Cloud Nine'

Shocked	Tired
Mouth Wide Open	Droppy Red Eyes
Eyes Popping Open	Yawning
Hands Covering Mouth	Trying To Keep Eyes Open
Jumping/Stepping Back	Slouching In Chair
Gasping For Air	Leaning Hands-On Head
Heart Beating Fast	Rubbing Eyes
	Stretching

Cold	Shy
Shivering	Blushing/Turns Red
Rubbing Hands Together	Looking Down
Hugging Self	Speaking Softly
Blowing On Hands	Arms Crossed
Seeing Breathe In The Air	Standing Away From Others
Eyes Watering/Tears	Hiding Behind Things
Freezing	
Lips Turning Blue	

Sad	Excited
Tears In Eyes	Mouth Wide Open
Trembling Lips Frown	Heart Pounding
Hanging Head Low	Jumping Up And Down
Dragging Feet	Clapping/Clasping Hands
Corners Of Lips Falls	
Looking Towards Floor	Eyes Wide Open
Shaky Quick Voice	Huge Smile Across Face

6.4 Lesson Plan:

Lesson Plan on Show not tell of Emotions

Objective: Students will learn how to Show not Tell in their creative writing

Introduction:

- Start with Induction. Have a game of Dumb Charades of a different version. Enact various emotions like Happy, Sad, Tired etc.
- Alternatively, you can use literature text as a reference to discuss how writers do show not tell.
- Share interesting video demonstrating show not tell.
- Let children guess the emotion. Then, initiate the discussion as to how did the guess the emotion. Ask them to identify which details helped them show, rather than tell, the emotion that the character was feeling.
- Gradually introduce them to the concept of Face, Body and Voice. **(FBV)**
- Write the sentence "She was Sad." on the chart paper. Ask students to think of ways they could show that she was sad, rather than just telling it.
- Write down their suggestions on the chart paper. For example, they might say that her eyes were red and puffy, or that she was slouching with her head down.
- Explain that using these sensory details can help create a more vivid and engaging story, and allow the reader to feel what the character is feeling.
- Give students examples of sentences that tell rather than show, such as "He was angry" or "She was happy."
- Ask students to brainstorm sensory details that would help them show, rather than tell, what the character was feeling. Write their ideas on the chart paper.

- Have students practice turning those sentences into descriptive paragraphs, using FBV details to show the emotion rather than telling it.
- As they work, circulate among the students, offering suggestions and guidance as needed.

Conclusion:

- Have students share their descriptive paragraphs with the class.
- Ask them to identify which details helped them show, rather than tell, the emotion that the character was feeling.
- Emphasize the importance of using descriptive details to create a more engaging and vivid story.
- Encourage students to continue practicing this skill in their writing.

SHOW NOT TELL IS INTEGRAL PART OF EVERY WRITING. IT HAS TO BE DONE FOR CHARACTER'S TRAIT, SETTING, CHARACTER'S ACTIONS AND EMOTIONS. IT ALSO HAS TO BE DONE FOR OBJECTS AND OTHER THINGS IN A STORY.

6.5 Sample Worksheets:

Don't Tell. Show!

Directions: On a separate sheet of paper, make the following "telling statements" show. You will change the sentences and add new things, but be sure to express the original idea.

Examples:

1. Telling: Tom didn't want to go to school today.

   Showing: Tom threw his books into his bag, crumpling his half-complete homework; he sighed.

2. Telling: Mike didn't want to go find the lost puppy.

   Showing: When Mike's mother asked him to find the lost puppy, Mike groaned, "Do I have to, Mom?"

3. Telling: Reading was Jay's favorite class.

   Showing: Jay waited the whole day to go to reading class and he always smiled when he got there.

1. I was really mad.

Show -

____

____

____

2. She was tired from having stayed up late.

Show -

____

____

____

3. Alec wasn't paying attention to the teacher.

Show -

____

____

____

4. He was bored while she was telling her story.

Show -

____

____

____

5. I was really happy.

Show -

____

____

____

6. Sammy was hungry.

Show -

____

____

____

____

Q2. Look at the following images and write 2-3 sentences showing the character's emotions:

1. _______________________________

____

____

____

2. _______________________________

____

____

____

3. _______________________________

____

____

____

____

4. _______________________________

____

____

____

____

5. _______________________________

____

____

____

____

Q3. In the following sentences, the book is *telling* you what the emotions are. You have to *show* the same emotions. The first one is already done for you:

Telling- Hugh was very happy.

Showing- Hugh grinned from ear to ear and began to giggle as he bounced joyfully into the yard.

1. My grandfather is sitting quietly in his chair.

____

____

____

2. His grandmother was angry at him.

____

____

____

3. The little boy was scared.

____

____

____

4. Karen was surprised to see her sister.

____

____

____

5. Rahil was shocked after listening to the story.

____

____

____

6.6 Sample Literature References:

1) Wilbur's heart pounded. He began to squeal. Then he raced in circles, kicking manure into the air. Then he turned a back flip. Then he planted his front feet and came to a stop in front of Charlotte's children.

– Charlotte's Web

2) Edwin was a bag of nerves as he stared at the Math paper. The ghost's threat to return nagged him. The questions got tangled like a twisted net in his head, leaving him chewing on his pencil most of the time.

– The Ghost of Malabar

3) "Charlie's eyes widened as he entered the chocolate factory. The sight of the flowing chocolate river and candy trees made his heart dance with joy."

– Charlie and the Chocolate factory

6.7 Links for reference:

https://youtu.be/YAKcbvioxFk

https://youtu.be/N4RthqSOcR0?si=vGFx6vZCLRoxrI9N

CHAPTER 7

IDIOMS AND PROVERBS

7.1 Introduction:

Idioms and proverbs enrich our language and make it more picturesque and beautiful.

An idiom is an expression or phrase that has a meaning of its own when taken together. This meaning is different from the actual meaning of the words.

Proverbs are short, wise sayings which are based on common sense and practical experience.

Observe:

Sammy was very tensed and nervous before his examination. He had worked really hard day and night. He knew he had to sacrifice some recreational things to get the desired results. He found certain subjects very easy and some he found difficult to study. In spite of his nervousness, he was confident of passing with good grades.

The same sentences may be re-written as follows:

Sammy was *bundle of nerves* (idiom)before his examination. He has been *burning the midnight oil* (idiom) for it. He realized no *pains, no gains* (proverb). He found certain subjects *as easy as a pie (simile)* and some *hard nut to crack* (idiom). In spite of his nervousness, he was confident of passing *with flying colours (*idiom*).*

Some examples of idioms:

- Tom was *shaking in his shoes*.
- The exhausted students *hit the sack*.
- At the party, Cindy felt *like a fish out of the water*.
- He has a very nice car, but he drives it *once in a blue moon*.

Some examples of proverbs:

- All that glitters is not gold.
- All work and no play make Jack a dull boy.
- Rome was not built in a day.
- Where there's a will, there's a way.

7.2 Idiom Banks

Group 1: Animal Idioms

⇒ Let the cat out of the bag
⇒ Hold your horses
⇒ Fish out of water
⇒ Raining cats and dogs
⇒ Cat nap
⇒ Ants in the pants

Group 2: Food Idioms

⇒ Break the ice
⇒ As cool as cucumber
⇒ Spill the beans
⇒ Couch potato
⇒ A piece of cake

Group 3: Weather Idioms

⇒ Under the weather
⇒ Raining cats and dogs

⇒ Weather the storm
⇒ On cloud nine
⇒ Blow hot and cold

Group 4: Colour Idioms

⇒ Green with envy
⇒ Red as a tomato
⇒ Out of the blue
⇒ White as a sheet
⇒ Tickled pink

Personality Idiom Bank:

⇒ All bark and no bite
⇒ The life of the party
⇒ A snake in the grass
⇒ A couch potato
⇒ A social butterfly
⇒ A tough cookie
⇒ A people person
⇒ A lone wolf

Cool as a Cucumber

7.3 Lesson Plan/ Induction Activities/ Teaching ideas:

1. Idioms can be wonderfully inducted with a help of Role- Play.

Sample role-play:

Characters:

Sam - a curious student

Alex - Sam's imaginative friend

Sam: Hey, Alex! I heard people using some funny phrases like "raining cats and dogs" or "break a leg." What do those mean?

Alex: Ah, Sam! Those are called idioms. They're like secret codes in language. Let's have some fun decoding them!

Sam: Cool! Can you explain the idiom "raining cats and dogs"?

Alex: Picture this, Sam. Imagine looking out the window, and instead of raindrops, you see fluffy cats and adorable dogs falling from the sky. But don't worry, it's just an expression! "Raining cats and dogs" actually means it's raining very heavily.

Sam: (giggles) That would be quite a sight! So, when someone says "break a leg," should I really break my leg?

Alex: Oh, no, Sam! Definitely not! "Break a leg" is just a way to wish someone good luck. It's like saying, "I hope you do your best and have a great performance." No broken bones involved; I promise!

Sam: Phew! That's a relief. But why do people say things that don't mean what they say?

Alex: Well, Sam, idioms add colour and humour to our language. They make conversations more interesting and playful.

Sam: (laughs) That would be crazy! So, can we make up our own idioms too?

Alex: Absolutely! Let's get creative, Sam. How about "tickled pink" to mean feeling really happy or "cat's pyjamas" to describe something cool or amazing? We can invent our own idioms and give our language a fun twist!

Sam: I love it, Alex! We can make our own secret language with these idioms. It's like having a superpower of words!

Alex: You got it, Sam! With idioms, we can add excitement and surprise to our conversations.

Sam: Thanks, Alex! I'm excited to start using idioms and discovering more of these funny phrases. Let's have fun decoding the secret language of idioms together!

Alex: Absolutely, Sam! Let's dive into the wonderful world of idioms and unravel their hidden meanings. It'll be an adventure of words!

2. It can alternatively be introduced by Mentor text or comparative text.

Sample 1: Sammy was very tensed and nervous before his examination. He had worked really hard day and night. He knew he had to sacrifice some recreational things to get the desired results. He found certain subjects very easy and some he found difficult to study. Inspite of his nervousness, he was confident of passing with good grades.

Sample 2: Sammy was *bundle of nerves* (idiom)before his examination. He has been *burning the midnight oil* (idiom) for it. He realized no *pains, no gains (*proverb*).* He found certain subjects *as easy as a pie (simile)* and some *hard nut to crack* (idiom). Inspite of his nervousness, he was confident of passing *with flying colours* (idiom).

3. Take sample texts from story books or video clips from popular TV shows like Young Sheldon.

Demonstrate the use of idioms.

Once upon a time in the bustling town of Meadowville, there lived a cheerful rabbit named Rusty. Rusty was as curious as a cat and often found himself in situations that made him the **talk of the town.** His friends, Lily the squirrel and Benny the bluebird, were always by his side, but Rusty had a habit of **jumping the gun and getting into hot water.**

One sunny day, Rusty decided to explore the mysterious old oak tree at the edge of the forest. Lily warned him **not to count his chickens before they hatched,** but Rusty was as stubborn as a mule. "I'll be back in a jiffy," he said, grinning from ear to ear.

As Rusty hopped closer to the tree, he noticed a shiny object glittering **like a diamond in the rough.** "Aha! This must be the treasure everyone talks about!" he exclaimed, feeling **like a kid in a candy store.** But before he could say "jackrabbit," the ground beneath him gave way, and he found himself in a hole as deep as the Grand Canyon.

"Oh, my stars and garters!" cried Benny, flying to the rescue with Lily. "Rusty, you've really **bitten off more than you can chew** this time!"

With teamwork and determination, they pulled Rusty out of the hole. As they dusted him off, Rusty realized the importance of **not counting his chickens before they hatch** and the value of having friends who always **had his back**.

From that day on, Rusty learned to **take things with a grain of salt** and think before leaping into unknown adventures. And although he still had a knack for finding trouble, his friends were there to lend a helping hand, proving that **every cloud has a silver lining**.

7.4 IDIOM Bank:

1. A blessing in disguise - something good that initially seemed bad
2. A dime a dozen - something that is very common
3. Add insult to injury - to make a bad situation even worse
4. Beat around the bush - to avoid saying something directly
5. Bite the bullet - to do something unpleasant that must be done
6. Best of both worlds - a situation that has all the advantages of two different things
7. Break a leg - good luck!
8. Bring home the bacon - to earn money to support your family
9. Burn the midnight oil - to study or work late at night
10. Call it a day - to stop working or doing something for the day
11. Can't judge a book by its cover - you can't tell what someone is like by their appearance
12. Cost an arm and a leg - to be very expensive

13. Cry over spilled milk - to regret something that has already happened

14. Cut corners - to do something quickly or cheaply, even if it means not doing it properly

15. Do or die - a situation in which you must do something or face serious consequences

16. Don't count your chickens before they hatch - don't assume that something will happen until it actually does

17. Easier said than done - something is more difficult to do than it is to say

18. Eat crow - to admit that you were wrong

19. Feel under the weather - to feel slightly ill

20. Get cold feet - to lose your courage at the last minute

21. Get your act together - to start organizing yourself and doing things properly

22. Give someone the cold shoulder - to ignore someone deliberately

23. Hit the nail on the head - to say or do something exactly right

24. Kill two birds with one stone - to achieve two things at the same time

25. Let the cat out of the bag - to reveal a secret

26. Let sleeping dogs lie - to avoid doing something that might cause problems

27. Once in a blue moon - very rarely

28. On cloud nine - to be very happy

29. Over the hill - getting old

30. Piece of cake - something very easy to do

31. Pull someone's leg - to joke with someone

32. Raining cats and dogs - raining very heavily

33. See eye to eye - to agree with someone

34. See red - to become very angry

35. Sell like hotcakes - to sell very quickly

36. Speak of the devil - someone you were just talking about suddenly appears

37. Steal someone's thunder - to take away someone's attention or excitement

38. Take a rain check - to postpone something until a later date

39. Take it easy - to relax and not worry

40. Talk someone's ear off - to talk to someone for a very long time

41. The ball is in your court - it is up to you to decide what to do next

42. The best things in life are free - the most valuable things in life cannot be bought with money

43. The early bird gets the worm - people who do things early are more likely to be successful

44. The grass is always greener on the other side - people often think that other people's lives are better than their own, even when they are not

45. The pen is mightier than the sword - words can be more powerful than weapons

46. There's no place like home - home is the best place to be

47. Think outside the box - to come up with new and creative ideas

48. Throw in the towel - to give up

49. Touch and go - a situation that is uncertain and could go either way

50. Under the weather - feeling slightly ill

51. Up in the air - undecided or uncertain

52. When in Rome, do as the romans do - when you are in a new place, you should adapt to the local customs

53. You can't teach an old dog new - it is difficult for people to change their habits or ways of thinking, especially as they get older

54. A penny for your thoughts. - I'm curious to know what you're thinking about.

55. Beat a dead horse. - to continue to talk or argue about something that has already been decided or is no longer important.

56. Break the ice. - to start a conversation or make someone feel more comfortable.

57. Can of worms. - a difficult or complicated situation that could cause a lot of problems if it is opened up.

58. Cat's got your tongue? - why are you so quiet?

59. We'll cross that bridge when we come to it - to deal with something when it happens rather than worrying about it before

60. Wild goose chase - a hopeless pursuit, something that is unattainable

61. Wouldn't be caught dead - dislike or would never do something

62. Wrap one's head around something - to understand something that is complicated or shocking

63. Sit on the fence - to adopt a position of compromise, take neither stance on an issue, not yes or no

64. Sit tight - to wait patiently

65. Sleep on it - to delay making a decision for a short period of time

66. Smell a rat - to suspect someone is a traitor, behaving illegally or is up to no good

67. So far, so good - to express satisfaction with how a situation is progressing

68. Spill the beans - to reveal information that was secret

69. Splash out - to spend a lot of money on something

70. Stab someone in the back - to betray or hurt someone who trusts you

71. Steal someone's thunder - to take attention or praise away from someone else's accomplishments by outdoing them with your own

72. Stick to one's guns - to refuse to change your mind or beliefs about something

73. Straight from the horse's mouth - information straight from the person who saw, heard or experienced the event

74. Taste of one's own medicine - when someone does something unpleasant and the same is wished on him/her

75. The last/final straw - the last in a series of bad things to happen, when your patience has run out

76. Through thick and thin - to continue to support someone even during difficult times

77. Time flies when you're having fun - when you're enjoying something time seems to move faster and you don't notice the passing of time

78. Twist someone's arm - to convince someone to do what you want them to

79. Pigs might fly - something that will never happen or is very unlikely

80. Pitch in - to join in, contribute or help with something

81. Play it by ear - to plan something in an improvised way (instead of planning ahead), deciding what to do as the plan develops

82. Pull oneself together - to regain control of your emotions after you've been upset, to calm down

83. No-brainer - an easy decision, something you don't need to think too hard about

84. Not one's cup of tea - something you don't like or are not interested in

85. Off the top of one's head - from memory, without a lot of thought or consideration

86. On the ball - to be alert, quick to understand and react to things

87. On the straight and narrow - to live in a way that is honest and moral, to stay out of trouble

88. Leave no stone unturned - to do everything you can to achieve something

89. Let someone off the hook - to avoid being punished for something or to avoid doing something

90. Hit the books - to start studying seriously

91. Hit the road - to leave somewhere or start a journey

92. Hit the sack - to go to bed in order to sleep

93. Hold your horses - another way of saying 'wait a moment' or 'don't rush'

94. Green fingers - to be good at gardening, able to make plants grow

95. Hang in there - to persist with something, to not give up

96. Have eyes in the back of one's head - to be able to see or sense what's going on all around you, when you can't physically see everything

97. Get up/out on the wrong side of bed - to wake up in a grumpy or bad mood for no obvious reason

98. Get off one's back - when someone won't stop criticising, bothering or telling you what to do

99. Get out of hand - to become difficult to control

100. Get over something - to overcome or move on from a difficult situation

7.5 Sample Worksheets:

Q1. Circle the idioms in the following sentences:

1. Sharon had butterflies in her stomach before the championship game.
2. My dad blew his stack when he saw my poor grades on my report card.
3. Jyoti was a bundle of nerves before getting her driving test results.
4. Last night, it was raining cats and dogs.
5. My parents rolled out the red carpet for our visiting relatives.
6. When I tried to get into the good school, the process involved a lot of red tape.
7. The athlete is as fit as a fiddle.
8. I am having a field day with my final exam.
9. The dog days of summer are starting to wear on me.
10. He was being a good Samaritan because he helped me out.

Q2. Read the idioms and write their meanings:

1. Fool's Paradise - __________________________________
2. Hand to mouth - __________________________________
3. Be on cloud nine - __________________________________
4. Once in a blue moon - __________________________________
5. Eat Humble Pie - __________________________________

Q3. Pick out the idioms and state their meanings. Also try to rewrite the passage using the meanings instead of the idioms:

Susan and Mike were as different as night and day. Susan was always the early bird, while Mike was a night owl. Despite their differences, they were like two peas in a pod, always supporting each other through thick and thin. Their friendship was a breath of fresh air in a world where people often keep their cards close to their chest. Together, they could weather any storm that came their way.

CHAPTER 8

PHRASAL VERBS

8.1 Understanding Phrasal Verbs:

Phrasal verbs are combinations of a verb and one or more particles (usually prepositions or adverbs) that together create a new, often idiomatic, meaning. The verb and particle work as a unit to convey a specific action or idea. Understanding their meaning can be challenging as it often goes beyond the literal meanings of individual words.

Examples of Phrasal Verbs:

Set off: It's not about putting something in motion but to trigger an event. "Her speech set off a wave of inspiration in the audience."

Enhancing Creative Writing:

Phrasal verbs are essential tools for creative writers, offering several advantages:

Imagery and Vivid Description: Phrasal verbs can bring a scene to life by creating vivid mental images.

For example, "The thunderstorm rolled in, casting a dark shadow over the city" paints a more compelling picture than saying "The thunderstorm arrived, darkening the city."

Character Development: The choice of phrasal verbs can reveal character traits and emotions.

"She tiptoed into the room" implies caution and secrecy, while "She stomped into the room" suggests anger and assertiveness.

Tone and Atmosphere: Phrasal verbs can set the tone and atmosphere of your story.

"The campfire crackled" evokes warmth and coziness, whereas "The fire roared" conveys danger and intensity.

Conciseness and Flow: Phrasal verbs often allow you to convey actions more concisely, improving the flow of your narrative.

Instead of saying "She made her way slowly up the hill," you can say "She trudged up the hill."

Incorporating Phrasal Verbs:

When incorporating phrasal verbs into your writing, remember to consider your target audience and the context of your story. Ensure that the meaning of the phrasal verb aligns with the narrative, and that it enhances, rather than complicates, your prose.

To summarise, phrasal verbs are versatile tools that can elevate your creative writing. By understanding their meanings and employing them judiciously, you can create good narratives and leave a lasting impression on your readers.

8.2 Phrasal Verbs List

Phrasal Verb	Meaning	Example Sentence
ask around	ask many people the same question	I asked around but nobody has seen my wallet.
add up to something	Equal	Your purchases add up to $205.32.
back something up	Reverse	You'll have to back up your car so that I can get out
back somebody up	Support	My wife backed me up over my decision to quit my job.
blow up	Explode	The racing car blew up after it crashed into the fence.

Phrasal Verb	Meaning	Example Sentence
break down	stop functioning (vehicle, machine)	Our car broke down at the side of the highway in the snowstorm.
break down	get upset	The woman broke down when the police told her that her son had died.
Break in	Force entry to a building	Somebody broke in last night and stole our stereo.
Break into something	Enter forcibly	The fireman had to break into the room to rescue the children.
Break something in	Wear something a few times so that it doesn't look/feel new	I need to break these shoes in before we run next week.
Break in	Interrupt	The TV station broke into report the news of the president's death.
Call something off	Cancel	Jason called the meeting off as he wasn't well.
Catch up	Get to the same point as somebody else	You'll have to run faster than that if you want to catch up with Marty.
Come across something	Find unexpectedly	I came across these old photos when I was tidying the closet.
Come apart	Separate	The top and bottom come apart if you pull hard enough.
Count on somebody/ something	Rely on	I am counting on you to make dinner while I am out.
Cross something out	Draw a line through	Please cross out your old address and write your new one.
Cut back on something	Consume less	My doctor wants me to cut back on sweets and fatty foods.
Cut in	Interrupt	Your father cut in while I was dancing with your uncle.

Phrasal Verb	Meaning	Example Sentence
Do something over	Do again	My teacher wants me to do my essay over because she doesn't like my topic.
Do away with something	Discard	It's time to do away with all of these old tax records.
Drop in/by/over	Come without an appointment	I might drop in/by/over for tea sometime this week.
Drop somebody/ something off	Take somebody/ something somewhere and leave them/it there	I have to drop my sister off at work before I come over.
Drop out	Quit a class, school etc	I dropped out of science because it was too difficult.
Fall apart	Break into pieces	My new dress fell apart in the washing machine.
Fall out	Separate from an interior	The money must have fallen out of my pocket.
Figure something out	Understand, find the answer	I need to figure out how to fit the piano and the bookshelf in this room.
Get something across/over	Communicate, make understandable	I tried to get my point across/over to the judge but she wouldn't listen.
Get along/on	Like each other	I was surprised how well my new girlfriend and my sister got along/on
Get around	Have mobility	My grandfather can get around fine in his new wheelchair.
Get away	Go on a vacation	We worked so hard this year that we had to get away for a week.
Get away with something	Do without being noticed or punished.	Jason always gets away with cheating in his Maths tests.
Get back	Return	We go back from our vacation last week.

Phrasal Verb	Meaning	Example Sentence
Get back at somebody	Retaliate, take revenge	My sister got back at me for stealing her shoes. She stole my favourite hat.
Get over something	Recover from an illness, loss, difficulty	I just got over the flu and now my sister has it.
Get over something	Overcome a problem	The company will have to close if it can't get over the new regulations.
Give something out	Give to many people (usually at no cost)	They were giving out free perfume samples at the department store.
Give something up	Quit a habit	I am giving up smoking as of January 1st
Give up	Stop trying	My maths homework was too difficult so I gave up
Go ahead	Start, proceed	Please go ahead and eat before the food gets cold.
Go over something	Review	Please go over your answers before you submit your test.
Go without something	Suffer lack or deprivation	When I was young, we went without winter boots.
Grow apart	Stop being friends over time	My best friend I grew apart after she changed schools
Grow back	Regrow	My roses grew back this summer.
Hand something in	Submit	I have to hand in my essay by Friday.
Hang in	Stay positive (informal)	Hang in there. I'm sure you'll find a job very soon.
Hang on	Wait a short time (informal)	Hang on while I grab my coat and shoes!
Hang up	End a phone call	He didn't say goodbye before he hung up.
Hold somebody/ something back	Prevent from doing/ going	I had to hold my dog back because there was a cat in the park.

Phrasal Verb	Meaning	Example Sentence
Hold something back	Hide an emotion	Jamie held back his tears at his grandfather's funeral.
Hold on	Wait a short time	Please hold on while I transfer you to the sales Department.
Look into something	Investigate	We are going to look into the price of snowboards today.
Look out for something/somebody	Be especially vigilant for	Don't forget to look out for snakes on the hiking trail.
Look something over	Check, examine	Can you look over my essay for spelling mistakes?
Look something up	Search and find information in a reference book or database	We can look her phone number up on the internet.
Look up to somebody	Have a lot of respect for	My little sister has always looked up to me.
Make something up	Invent, lie about something	Josie made up a story about why we were late.
Pass away	Die	His uncle passed away last night after a long illness.
Pass out	Faint	It was so hot in the church that an elderly lady passed out.
Put up with somebody/something	Tolerate	I don't think I can put up with three small children in the car.
Put something on	Put clothing/ accessories on your body	Don't forget to put on your new earrings for the party.
Run into somebody/ something	Meet unexpectedly	I ran into an old school – friend at the mall.
Run over somebody/ something	Drive a vehicle over a person or thing	I accidentally ran over your bicycle in the driveway.

Phrasal Verb	Meaning	Example Sentence
Take after somebody	Resemble a family member	I take after my mother. We are both impatient.
Take something apart	Purposely break into pieces	He took the car breaks apart and found the problem.
Take something back	Return an item	I have to take our new TV back because it doesn't work.
Take off	Start to fly	My lane takes off in five minutes.

CHAPTER 9

ESSAY WRITING

9.1 What is an Essay?

An essay is a short piece of writing which is set around a specific topic or subject. The piece of writing will give information surrounding the topic but will also display the opinions and thoughts of the author.

Classification of Essays

Essays may be classified as Narrative Essays, Descriptive Essays, Expository Essays, Reflective Essays and Imaginative Essays.

1. **Narrative Essays** – A narrative essay consists mainly in the narration of some event, or series of events.
2. **Descriptive Essays** – A descriptive essay consists of a description of some person, place or thing.
3. **Expository Essays** – An expository (or explanatory) essay consists of an exposition or explanation of some subject.
4. **Imaginative Essays** – Essays on subjects such as the feelings and experiences of the sailor wrecked on a desert island may be called imaginative Essays. In such the writer is called to place himself in imagination in a position of which he has had no actual experience. Such subjects as "If I were a king," or "The autobiography of a horse," would call for imaginative essays.
5. **Argumentative Essay:** Argumentative essays present a specific point of view or argument and provide evidence to support it. The goal is to persuade the reader to agree with the author's perspective.

6. **Persuasive Essay**: Similar to argumentative essays, persuasive essays aim to convince the reader of a particular viewpoint. However, they may use emotional appeals in addition to evidence and logic.

9.2 Writing the Essay

Structure of an Essay – We may divide an essay into three parts – the introduction, the body of the Essay, and the Conclusion.

(a) The Introduction – This, in a short essay, must be very brief. It would be absurd to have the porch bigger than the building itself. It may be simply a sentence, or a very short paragraph. But it should always be arresting and pertinent to the subject. The introduction may consist of a definition or a quotation, proverb, very brief story, or general remark, leading up to the subject.

(b) The Body of the essay – This is really the essay itself – the house to which the introduction is the front door, and the conclusion the back door, or exit.

- In arranging the body of the essay observe proportion; that is, let each part have due weight given to it. If the subject is "The good and bad influence of Newspapers," do not devote three-quarters of the essay to good influences and so leave only a quarter for the bad. Closely follow your full outline throughout.

- The paragraphs should be well constructed and should be related to one another according to the direction of your outline; and, as far as possible, the connection between one and another should be shown.

- Take pains in selecting words and phrases which exactly express the ideas which you have in mind and frame your sentences so that they are quite clear and forceful.

- Avoid the use of unnecessary words. In revising your essay, look out for useless repetitions and redundant expressions, and strike them out.

- Match the words to the sense, and adapt the style to the subject-matter. Do not write frivolously on a serious subject, or ponderously on a light and humorous subject.

(c) The Conclusion – As the introduction should arouse interest, the conclusion should satisfy it. An effective and satisfying end to an essay is as important as an arresting beginning. An abrupt or feeble ending may spoil the whole effect of the essay.

A good conclusion may consist of –

(a) a summing up of the arguments of the essay; (b) final conclusion drawn from the subject-matter; (c) a suitable quotation; (d) a sentence that strikingly expresses the main point you want to drive home.

To sum up:

1. Clearly define your subject in your own mind.
2. Think over it, until ideas about it come into your mind, and jot the points down on paper as they occur to you – numbering them.
3. Classify these points in groups under suitable headings, rejecting any that are unsuitable.
4. Arrange these headings in a bare outline.
5. Fill in the outline, making a full outline.
6. Now begin to write the essay, dividing it into paragraphs.
7. The essay should consist of introduction, body and conclusion.

   (a) Make the introduction arresting.

   (b) Keep the parts of the body of the essay in proper proportion; and take pains in choosing words, constructing sentences and building up paragraphs.

   (c) Make the conclusion effective and satisfying.

8. Write in a simple, concise, clear, direct and natural style.

CHAPTER 10

DESCRIPTIVE ESSAY

10.1 Introduction:

WHAT IS THE DESCRIPTIVE WRITING?

Descriptive writing is a vivid and detailed account, or observation of a person, a place, a memory, an event, or an object. In simple terms, descriptive writing can be practically defined as "Show, Don't Tell".

➤ When the writer has to skilfully depict a certain object, situation or person in such a vivid manner that the readers is able to visualize it in his/her mind, it is a descriptive composition. It could be of a person, place, event or an object.

Important ingredients:

1. Show instead of tell: Create a vivid picture in words with the help of five senses. Do not limit yourself to only what you see. Include what you hear, smell, taste and feel too.

E.g., If you are describing A DAY IN THE FOREST:

See: The trees rose high into the sky. A rabbit scampered into its hole. The forest was so dense, that it looked dark and scary in the distance.

Sound: The monkeys were chattering in the distance while birds twittered in the trees. The grass swished under our feet. Suddenly we heard the loud, threatening roar in the distance.

Smell: The air smelt fresh, wet earth. The fragrance of wild forest was enchanting. The aroma of the grass was so different.

Taste: I felt thirsty and we drank from the nearby stream where the water tasted bland, pure and fresh. We the ate wild berries that were sweet and tangy at the same time.

Touch: The stones felt rough under my feet and soon my feet fell sore after five minutes of walking on the bare earth. Mosquitoes stung viciously but the gentle breeze patted my face and that helped me for a while.

2. Use descriptive vocabulary: Use adjectives, verbs, idioms, and figures of speech such as similes and metaphors to make essay more interesting.

> E.g., Her blue and copper coloured hair made her feel like fish water.

3. Use comparisons: Feel free to compare objects, scenes and make people to make details more vivid and easy to imagine.

> E.g., She was walking like an ant, climbing the stairs slowly and with immense difficulty.

4. Precise language. General adjectives, nouns, and passive verbs are used sparingly. Instead, specific adjectives and nouns and strong action verbs give life to the picture being painted in the reader›s mind.

5. Thoughtful organization. Some ways to organize descriptive writing include: chronological (time), spatial (location), and order of importance. Descriptive writing about a person might begin with a physical description, followed by how the person thinks, feels and acts.

6. Vivid details. Specific details paint a picture in the reader's mind and appeal to the reader›s senses. Descriptive writing may also go beyond creating a strong sensory impression to give the reader a "picture" of the feelings the description evokes in the writer.

Title: "The Enchanted Forest"

As Jenny wandered through the dense forest, she was captivated by the twinkling fairy lights that adorned the trees. The leaves whispered secrets as they rustled in the breeze, and the air was thick with the scent of pine and moss. She felt a tingling in her toes and a flutter in her heart, as if the forest was whispering a magical invitation just for her. With wide-eyed wonder, she followed the trail, eager to discover the secrets that awaited her in the enchanted forest.

7. Figurative language. Tools of the writer's craft such as analogy, simile, metaphor and personification add depth to authors' descriptions.

The ocean roared like a fierce beast, its waves crashing against the shore with a primal rhythm. The salty mist hung in the air like a fine veil, kissing the skin with a briny tang. The sun danced on the water's surface like a scattering of diamonds, casting a dazzling display of light and colour.

A: The description of an object:

1. The class and category of objects.
2. The shape, size, colour, material etc.
3. Comparison to other things.
4. Features and Utility.

E.g., Swings, Mobile phones, Clouds etc.

Description of a mobile phone:

I hold the sleek mobile phone in my hand, feeling its smooth and cool surface against my fingertips. The device emits a subtle, pleasant scent, like a faint whiff of newness. As I power it on, I hear a soft chime and the gentle vibration of the phone coming to life. The screen displays vibrant colours, and as I swipe my finger across it, I feel a slight resistance under my touch. The phone emits a series of satisfying clicks and taps as I navigate through its various features. When I make a call, I hear the clear sound of the other person's voice coming through the speaker, crisp and distinct. The phone also offers a variety of ringtones and notifications, each with their own unique sound. Overall, the mobile phone engages my senses, combining its sleek design, subtle scent, tactile feedback, and auditory cues to create a modern and interactive experience.

B. The description of a scene usually comprises of:

- A general impression of scene.
- Wh and How questions.
- Five senses- (Sight, sound, smell, Taste, Feel)
- Describe people who are part of the scene.
- Prior memories associated related to scene.
- Brilliant Vocabulary.

E.g., A beautiful garden, A village, One winter morning. The city at night etc.

Sample Essay on View Outside My window

My room is located on the eighth floor of the apartment complex, overloading a peaceful back alley with tress and several high rises in the background, creating a picture of a city with the past and present colliding. There is a tall palm tree directly outside my window which sways wildly in the monsoon season. I can see far into the city if I climb to the top of my bunk bed. The sun in the sky always provides a beautiful shade to the scene. I live close to the main road of the area, so during all times of the day, there is the sound of muffled traffic and busy streets. The streets are filled with tress, their green heads poking out from across terraces, making the roads feel like a sea of leaves.

Early in the morning, when I wake up to get ready for school, the sun is just rising in the distance. The sky is a mesh of blue and black and wispy clouds are visible. The moon looks like a tiny faded circle as the sun's light fills the area. A small breeze blows through, causing the leaves to rustle, the sound pleasantly harmonizing with the early bird chirps. It's very cool in the mornings and has a pleasant atmosphere. The view is hardly visible due to less light, but still lovely all the same. It smells like petrichor, even when it hasn't rained. Afternoon has a hazy hum in the air, light traffic and harsh sun throwing everything into sharp relief. It is extremely warm and even more humid in the monsoon. It is mostly silent and almost no breeze. I can smell smoke from the cars in the air and not much of nature in the air. It isn't my favourite time of the day but the leaves look lovely in the sunlight.

Late in the evening is my favourite time of the day. I love to study next to my window, with the pleasant and cool atmosphere, the peachy hues of the sky with tins of black on the horizon. There is a sweet breeze and the soft sounds of evening traffic come through. I play soft music which enhances the scene. The sunlight reflects off the window of the high rises in amazing ways, giving the effect of sunlight on waves at the beach. The sun is also gentle and it is easy to just stare at the view. The moon soon makes a tiny appearance as the evening comes to a close. The leaves rustle every now and then, and if you watch the skyline for long enough, you can see several bats across. It is a beautiful time of day and the optimum time for just staring out of the window. I relish the simple pleasure of sipping my coffee while seated by the window, indulging in the soothing embrace of the fresh, invigorating breeze.

At night, it's hard to see anything, but during Diwali, the whole view lights up, hundreds upon thousands of lights adorning the night, building draped in strings of bright colours and warm lanterns. The whole view is so colourful, it's hard to look away.

My room has the best view in the house, and I often just sit by window, whiling away the time by staring outside my window and enjoying the breeze. It is lovely view; one I hope to enjoy for many months to come.

C. The description of a person usually comprises of:

- The name of the person and writer's relationship with her.
- Physical features: The height, looks body shape, stature.
- Clothing, posture, speech, mannerisms.
- Life history, family background.
- His/her opinions, interests and actions.
- What others say about him/her.
- How he/she affects other people.
- Why you like or dislike her.

E.g., The person I admire the most. My favourite sportsperson, My father etc.

10.2 Lesson Plan

Writing a descriptive essay involves creating a vivid and detailed picture of a person, place, object, or event. The goal is to engage the reader's senses and emotions by providing a rich and immersive experience.

Here's a basic format to help you structure your descriptive essay:

➢ Introduction:

- Begin with a strong hook to grab the reader's attention.
- Provide some background information about the subject of your essay.

➢ Body Paragraphs:

- Organize your body paragraphs based on specific aspects or features of the subject.

- Use sensory details (sight, sound, touch, taste, smell) to create a vivid and immersive experience for the reader.
- Show, don't tell. Instead of simply stating facts, use descriptive language and imagery to evoke emotions and create a strong impression.
- Arrange details in a logical order, such as from the most prominent to the least prominent or in a chronological sequence.
- Transition smoothly between paragraphs to maintain a cohesive flow.

➢ Conclusion:

- Summarize the main points and restate the thesis in a fresh way.
- Leave a lasting impression on the reader by reinforcing the significance of the subject or reflecting on its impact.
- Avoid introducing new information in the conclusion.
- Editing and Revising:
- Review your essay for clarity, coherence, and consistency.
- Check for grammatical and spelling errors.
- Ensure that your language is precise and evocative.
- Ask someone else to read your essay and provide feedback.

➢ Descriptive Techniques:

- Use vivid and specific language to create a sensory-rich experience for the reader.
- Appeal to the five senses (sight, sound, touch, taste, smell) to paint a comprehensive picture.
- Employ figurative language, such as similes and metaphors, to enhance your descriptions.
- Consider the overall mood and tone of your essay and adjust your language accordingly.

Remember, the key to a successful descriptive essay is to engage the reader's imagination and make them feel as if they are experiencing the subject firsthand. Experiment with language and be creative in expressing your observations and emotions.

Sample Essay on: My Grandmother

In my life, there is one person who has a special place in my heart and has always been a guiding light for me - my beloved grandmother. She is an extraordinary woman who has left an indelible mark on my life with her unwavering love, wisdom, and compassion.

My grandmother stands at a modest height, her frame slightly stooped by the weight of the years she carried with grace. Her skin, weathered by the passage of time, bore the fine lines of wisdom and experience, each wrinkle telling a story of a life well-lived. Her eyes, the windows to her soul, were a deep and warm shade of hazel, with a wisdom that surpassed her years. They twinkled with a mischievous glint when she shared stories from her youth and softened with tenderness when she spoke of family and the values she held dear. She always wears her silver hair into a pulled back neat bun, adorned with a simple hairpin or two. And her voice was soft and soothing, like a gentle lullaby.

One particular incident that left a lasting impression on me was when I was going through a tough time during my teenage years. I was struggling with self-doubt and feeling overwhelmed by the challenges I was facing. My grandmother noticed the change in my demeanour and gently pulled me aside for a heart-to-heart conversation.

With her warm and caring demeanour, she patiently listened to my concerns without judgment. She offered words of comfort and reassurance, reminding me of my worth and potential. She shared her own experiences of overcoming adversity and encouraged me to persevere with resilience and determination. Her unwavering belief in me and her unconditional love provided me with the strength and confidence I needed to face my challenges head-on.

My grandmother's words of wisdom and encouragement were a turning point in my life. Her faith in me instilled a renewed sense of self-confidence and helped me navigate through difficult times with courage and determination. Her unconditional love and support never wavered, and I knew that I could always count on her to be there for me, no matter what.

Apart from that incident, my grandmother's constant presence in my life has been a source of comfort and guidance. She has always been my pillar of strength, providing me with valuable advice, sharing her life experiences, and cheering me on in my pursuits. Her wisdom and compassion have helped shape my character and values, and I am grateful for the positive impact she has had on my life.

My grandmother's talents and creativity have also left a lasting impression on me. I remember spending countless hours with her in her beautiful garden, learning about different plants, and helping her tend to them. Her patience and expertise in gardening inspired my own love for nature and nurtured my appreciation for the beauty of the world around me.

Furthermore, her culinary skills have left an indelible mark on my taste buds. I cherish the memories of baking pies, kneading dough, and cooking up delicious meals in her kitchen. Her creativity in the kitchen has sparked my own love for cooking and experimenting with flavours, and I often find myself trying to recreate her signature recipes.

In conclusion, my beloved grandmother has had a profound impact on my life, and she remains my favourite person. Her unwavering love, wisdom, creativity, and selflessness continue to inspire me to be the best version of myself. The particular incident of her comforting and guiding me during a difficult time left a lasting impression on me and has shaped me into the person I am today. I am incredibly grateful for the privilege of having her in my life, and I will always treasure the memories and lessons she has shared with me.

10.3 Lesson Plan/Induction Activities:

Materials Needed:

- ➢ Whiteboard and markers
- ➢ Sample descriptive essays

Objectives:

- ➢ Students will understand the concept of descriptive writing.
- ➢ Students will identify the key elements of a descriptive essay.
- ➢ Students will draft their own descriptive essays using sensory details.

Step-by-Step Format:

Introduction (10 minutes):

Begin by discussing what descriptive writing is and why it's important. Explain that descriptive writing paints a vivid picture in the reader's mind.

- ➢ Introduction: Sets the scene or context.
- ➢ Thesis statement: Conveys the main impression or emotion.
- ➢ Body paragraphs: Describe the subject in detail using sensory language (Five senses).
- ➢ Conclusion: Summarizes main points and add a conclusion which explains the readers the impact of the scene.

- ❖ Show a sample descriptive essay or paragraph to the class. Read it aloud, and discuss the sensory language used in the example.
- ❖ Discuss the importance of engaging the reader's five senses.
- ❖ Guide students in selecting a subject to describe (e.g., a favourite place, a cherished possession, or a memorable experience).

- ❖ Help students brainstorm sensory details related to their chosen subject. Write these details on the whiteboard.
- ❖ Independent Writing Assignment
- ❖ Assign students to write a descriptive paragraph/essay about their chosen subject using the sensory details they brainstormed. Remind them to include an introduction, a thesis statement, and sensory descriptions in their paragraphs.
- ❖ Conclusion and Reflection: Conclude the lesson with a class discussion about the importance of descriptive writing and the impact of sensory details on the reader's experience.

Here's a sample descriptive paragraph about a busy city street:

The bustling city street teemed with life and energy. People hurriedly walked in every direction, their footsteps creating a symphony of hurried rhythms. Cars in a rainbow of colours inched forward, their horns occasionally blaring in impatient harmony. The scent of street food wafted from bustling food carts, mixing with the exhaust fumes and the subtle fragrance of coffee from a nearby café. Neon signs illuminated the pavement, advertising the latest products and services, casting a vibrant glow that competed with the fading daylight. Towering skyscrapers framed the scene, their reflective glass surfaces mirroring the chaotic yet captivating dance of urban existence. Amidst the noise and commotion, the city street remained a testament to the ceaseless movement and diversity that defined metropolitan life.

Engaging activities are essential when teaching descriptive essay writing to make the learning process more enjoyable and effective. Here are some activities to kickstart your lessons:

1. **Observation Walk:** Take your students on an observation walk around the school campus or a nearby park. Encourage them to use all their senses to observe and note down details about their surroundings. Later, in the classroom, have them share their

observations and discuss how they can use these details in their writing.

2. **Sensory Bags:** Prepare several bags with items that engage the senses, like a feather, a small citrus fruit, a piece of rough fabric, etc. Students pick a bag and describe the item inside using sensory language. This activity helps them practice incorporating sensory details into their writing.

3. **Picture Prompts**: Show students a series of interesting or unusual pictures. Ask them to write a descriptive paragraph based on what they see in the pictures. This activity stimulates their imagination and helps them create vivid descriptions.

4. **Descriptive Object Box**: Fill a box with random objects (e.g., a seashell, a toy, a vintage key) and have students draw one item from the box. They must then write a descriptive paragraph about the object, including its appearance, texture, and any emotions or memories it may evoke.

5. **Sensory Stations**: Set up various sensory stations around the classroom, such as a bowl of fragrant flowers, a sound recording of rain, or a piece of velvet fabric. Have students rotate through the stations, making notes on the sensory experiences. Later, they can use these notes to write descriptive paragraphs.

6. **Travel Brochure**: Provide students with a blank "travel brochure" template for a made-up location. In their groups, they must create a descriptive travel brochure for this location, including enticing descriptions of the scenery, activities, and local culture.

7. **Mystery Box:** Place a hidden object in a box and describe it to the class without revealing what it is. Students then write a descriptive paragraph based on your description. Afterward, reveal the object and discuss how well their descriptions matched the reality.

8. **Comparative Descriptions**: Give students a list of pairs of related objects (e.g., a rose and a daisy, a mountain and a hill). Have them

write a paragraph comparing and contrasting the two objects using sensory language.

9. **Guest Speaker**: Invite a guest speaker, such as a local author or a nature expert, to discuss the importance of descriptive writing and share their experiences. This provides real-world context and inspiration for students.

10. **Descriptive Essay "Show and Tell"**: Ask students to bring an object from home that is important to them. During a "Show and Tell" session, they describe their object using sensory details, explaining why it's meaningful. This helps them practice descriptive writing with a personal touch.

You can tweak the activities to suit the age -group or grade that you are teaching.

Remember to encourage creativity and imagination while teaching descriptive writing. These engaging activities will not only make the learning process enjoyable but also improve your students' descriptive writing skills.

10.4 Banks:

1. My first Bicycle
2. My Hobby
3. A journey to the hills
4. The noisy neighbour
5. A road accident
6. My favourite dish
7. A day's shopping
8. An unforgettable evening
9. Your city on a festive evening
10. A dream that came true
11. My best childhood memories
12. A special day in my life

13. The day everything went wrong
14. An interesting book (This should have the name of the book, the author, the story or subject matter in short and what you like about the book)
15. A cricket match I enjoyed (This should include all the details of the match and what you liked about it and why)
16. The best mistake I ever made
17. A rainy day
18. A morning walk
19. Republic Day celebrations
20. An ideal student
21. Sports day in my school
22. A visit to an Exhibition
23. An evening at a railway station
24. Your first visit to a beach or the mountains
25. The last major festival that you celebrated – write about how you spent the day, whom you met, the special things you did that day, the food you ate or gifts that you gave/received, and whatever you enjoyed it.
26. The view from moving passenger train.
27. Describe a cozy reading nook or corner. Include details about the comfortable seating, soft lighting, and the books or items that make it a perfect place for relaxation and reading.
28. A Summer Carnival: Describe the atmosphere and attractions of a summer carnival. Depict the bright colours, the sounds of laughter and music, and the excitement of the rides and games.
29. A Busy Traffic Junction. Describe the Scene. Sights and sounds and how did it make you feel.
30. Pandemonium at the picnic (A picnic or excursion is an enjoyable experience if shared, especially if something exciting takes place. Describe such an occasion
31. The person you admire the most

10.5 Sample worksheets:

My Visit to an amusement park

Plan your essay- (Use Wh and how, five senses and brilliant words, make three paragraphs.)

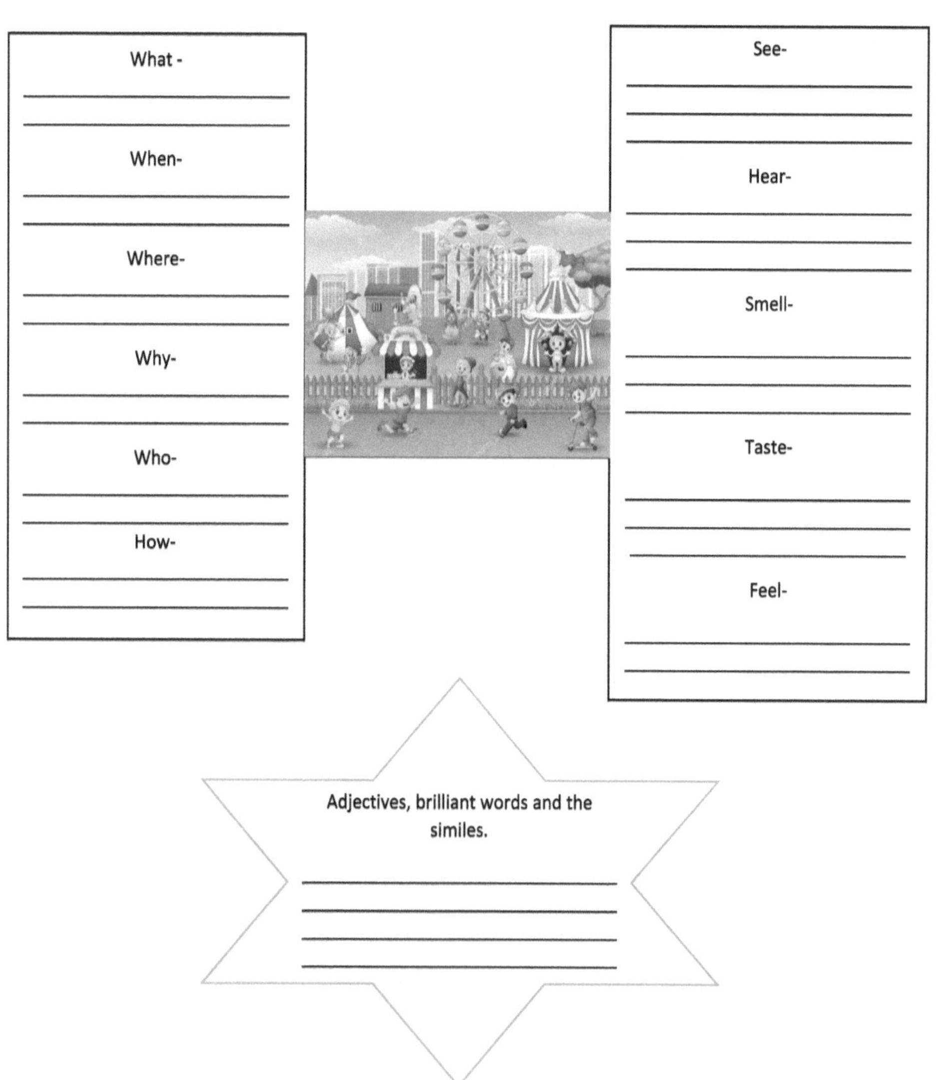

A Day at the Park

Plan your essay- (Use Wh and how, five senses and brilliant words, make three paragraphs.)

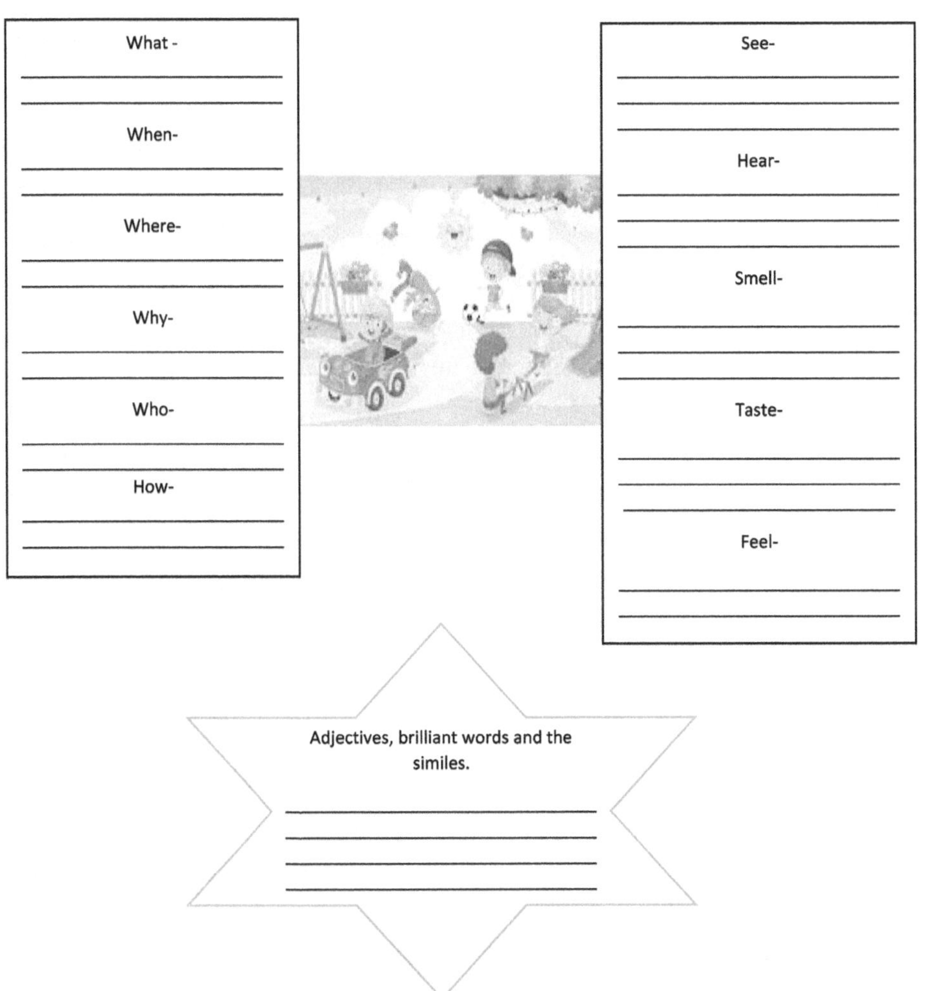

10.6 Sample Literature References:

1. Harry Potter and the Philosopher's Stone

Feeling oddly as though his legs had turned to lead, Harry got into line behind a boy with sandy hair, with Ron behind him, and they walked out of the chamber, back across the hall and through a pair of double doors into the Great Hall.

Harry had never even imagined such a strange and splendid place. It was lit by thousands and thousands of candles which were floating in midair over four long tables, where the rest of the students were sitting. These tables were laid with glittering golden plates and goblets. At the top of the hall was another long table where the teachers were sitting. Professor McGonagall led the first-years up here so that they came to a half in a line facing the other students, with the teachers behind them. The hundreds of faces staring at them looked like pale lanterns in the flickering candlelight. Dotted here and there around the students, the ghosts shone misty silver. Mainly to avoid all the staring eyes, Harry looked upwards and saw a velvety black ceiling dotted with stars. He heard Hermione whisper, "It's bewitched to look like the sky outside, I read it in Hogwarts: A History."

It was hard to believe there was a ceiling there at all, and that the Great Hall didn't simply open on to the heavens.

Harry quickly looked down again as Professor McGonagall silently placed a four-legged stool in front of the first-years. On top of the stool, she put a pointed wizard's hat. This hat was patched and frayed and extremely dirty. Aunt Petunia wouldn't have let it in the house.

2. The Hobbit

In a hole in the ground there lived a hobbit. Not a nasty, dirty, wet hole, filled with the ends of worms and an oozy smell, nor yet a dry, bare sandy hole with nothing in it to sit down on or eat: it was a hobbit-hole, and that means comfort.

It had a perfectly round door like a porthole, painted green with a shiny yellow brass knob in the exact middle. The door opened on to a tube-shaped hall like a tunnel: a very comfortable tunnel without smoke, with paneled walls, and floors tiled and carpeted, provided with polished chairs and lots and lots of pegs for hats and coats—the hobbit was fond of visitors.

The tunnel wound on and on, going fairly but not quite straight into the side of the hill—The Hill, as all the people for many miles around called it—and many little round doors opened out of it, first on one side and then on another. No going upstairs for the hobbit: bedrooms, bathrooms, cellars, pantries (lots of these), wardrobes (he had whole rooms devoted to clothes), kitchens, dining-rooms, all were on the same floor, and indeed on the same passage.

The best rooms were all on the left-hand side (going in) for these were the only ones to have windows—deep-set round windows looking over his garden and meadows beyond, sloping down to the river.

This hobbit was a very well-to-do hobbit, and his name was Baggins. The Baggins had lived in the neighbourhood of The Hill for time out of mind.

10.7 Links for reference:

How to write descriptively – by Nalo Hopkinson on Ted Ed You Tube

https://jerichowriters.com/sense-of-place-novel/

Jon Gingerich writes:

https://litreactor.com/columns/writing-powerful-descriptions

Mary Jaksch writes:

https://writetodone.com/how-to-write-better-descriptions/

Here are some websites that can help you with teaching descriptive essay writing:

1. <u>Reading Rockets:</u> This website provides a comprehensive guide to teaching descriptive writing. It includes routines and structures for teaching descriptive writing, such as chronological (time), spatial (location), and order of importance. It also provides examples of effective instruction in descriptive writing.

2. <u>Just Add Students:</u> This website offers easy ways to teach descriptive writing. It includes mini-lessons on identifying descriptive writing, finding descriptive texts, and creating a collection of descriptive writing examples.

3. <u>CollegeEssay.org:</u> This website provides free descriptive essay examples that can help you understand how to explain the plot, characters, setting, and the entire theme effectively.

Strategies to keep in mind while doing descriptive writing:

1. Imagine you're right there with the characters and use the five senses (sight, sound, touch, taste, and smell) to help readers experience the scene. Share only the details that matter for the story.

2. Choose your words carefully. Use good adjectives and nouns, but don't use too many. Too many descriptions can make the story slow and boring.

3. Use strong action words (verbs) that don't need extra words (adverbs). Avoid using "am," "is," "are," "was," and "were" when you can.

4. Only include descriptions that help the reader picture what's happening. Don't add details just to make the story longer.

5. Try to create a sense of drama, wonder, and curiosity in your writing. Descriptions can turn regular writing into something beautiful that captures the reader's heart.

6. Read your favourite authors, whether they write fiction or nonfiction, and pay attention to how they tell their stories. Notice how much description they use, what interesting words they choose, and whether you feel like you're right there in the story with the main character.

CHAPTER 11

CHARACTER DESCRIPTION

11.1 Introduction:

An essay or story revolves around characters and the situations they get into. Hence, describing the character is of prime importance to him or her come alive and connect with the reader.

Thus, it is important to learn the:

a. physical features
b. clothes and accessories
c. traits

Hair	bald patch, bouncy, braided, grey, plaited, punk-style, streaked, lustrous, knotted, pony-tail, grey-haired
Forehead	narrow, broad, scarred, shining, wrinkled, with worry lines
Eyebrow	arched, bushy, raised, knit, shapely, sparse
Eyes	almond-eyed, blood-shot eyes, drowsy, fiery, squinting, drowsy, beady big
Nose	bloated, flared, hooked, pudgy, pointed, long
Lips	pouting, quivering, rosy, trembling, thick
Teeth	chipped, dirty, even, golden, missing, pearly-white, toothless, uneven, stained
Jaw	bony, clenched, drooping, sagging, angular
Cheeks	chubby, dimpled, high-boned, hollow, rosy
Chin	bearded, square

Skin	dry, freckled, oily, rashes, wrinkled, smooth, freckled, spotted
Special or unusual marks	big mole, broken nose, cleft lip, cross- eyed, extra thumb, dwarf-like, stammering, tattoos.
Complexion	dark, fair, whiteish, rosy, peachy
Body build	thin, fat, plump, medium built, muscular, dwarfish, slim, short, lanky
Mannerisms	nervous, shifty-eyed, sniffling, nail biting, licking lips, rubbing hands, tapping feet, eye twitch

CLOTHES

The attire adds to the personality of the character hence, equipping oneself with good vocabulary pertaining to apparel is very important.

Garments	jackets, coats, trouser, shorts, suits, skirts, dresses, sweaters, waistcoats, sportswear, jogging suit, swimsuit, swimming trunks, tracksuit, jeans, pyjamas
Footwear	boots, slippers, platforms, sandals, sneakers, stilettos, trainers
Headgear and Scarves	bandana, Gandhi cap, hat, helmet, hood, muffler, turban, bonnet
Accessories	bags, bangles, belt, brooch, glasses, gloves, hair bands, hair clips, hand bag, handkerchief, jewellery, keychains, mittens, necklace, nose ring, ribbons
Clothes condition	fashionable, crumpled, ironed, ragged, dirty, shabby, loose-fitting, silky, smooth
Clothes pattern	checked, flowery, polka-dotted, pin-stripped

TRAITS

Characters will have qualities which shapes the plot of the story. Giving them appropriate qualities as per your plot is of utmost importance.

The character can have positive as well as negative traits.

Positive Traits (Qualities)

Able	Bright	Dreamer	Fair
Active	Brilliant	Dynamic	Familiar
Adorable	Broad-minded	Easy-going	Incredible
Ambitious	Busy	Ecstatic	Innocent
Attractive	Calm	Effective	Innovative
Awesome	Dependable	Enthusiastic	Intelligent
Brave	Determined	Excited	Jovial
Benevolent	Disciplined	Experienced	Joyful

Keen	Handsome	Patriotic	Rich
Kind	Happy	Pleasant	Respectful
Lovable	Helpful	Positive	Smart
Loyal	Hopeful	Popular	Satisfied
Loving	Imaginative	Pretty	Shy
Mature	Obedient	Productive	Sincere
Mischievous	Open-minded	Remarkable	Strong
Neat	Optimistic	Responsible	spirited

Studious			
Successful			
Versatile			
Vivacious			
Well- organized			
Witty			

Negative traits (qualities)

Aggressive	Evil	Lazy	Whimsical
Angry	Embarrassed	Sad	Wild

Arrogant	Fearful	Snobbish	
Anxious	Guilty	Spineless	
Bashful	Hateful	Stubborn	
Bossy	Helpless	Timid	
Boastful	Insane	Ugly	
Churlish	Irresponsible	Unreliable	
Conceited	Jealous	Unskilled	
Confused	Naïve	Untrustworthy	
Cruel	Nasty	Vacant	
Dominant	Negative	Vain	
Dull	Pitiful	Violent	
Disgusted	Poor	Weak	
Dangerous	Rude	Wild	

Here are some more examples of descriptions of physical features. Notice how adding a detail of action, to the character being described, makes a difference.

11.2 Example:

a. George, who was the most interesting member of the smith family, was actually Georgina. Her cropped, chestnut coloured hair and slim, athletic body often made people think that she was a boy. On top of that, she usually wore jeans, an ancient t-shirt and a scowl on her face.

b. Mr. Rajpal was called the Pied Piper of Pedder Road. He mesmerized children with his warm, teddy-bear like appearance; his bag of never-ending stories; and the love that enveloped them whenever they met him. At 55, Mr. Rajpal was cheerfully plump. The children loved playing with his salt-and-pepper beard, and running their hands through his greying hair.

More examples–

1. <u>Diana - the pretty maiden</u>

Diana is pretty. She has wavy lustrous waist-length hair. Her broad forehead and her shapely eyebrows highlight her spectacular face. She has rosy cheeks, twinkling blue eyes and a pointed nose that has charmed many. Her pearly white teeth and smooth skin make all the maidens green with envy.

2. <u>Taruna- the house help</u>

Taruna Didi helps my mother with her housework. She is tall and fair. She has beautiful bright eyes and chubby cheeks like apples. She loves to dress up in colourful clothes. Ribbons adorn her long hair and her glass bangles twinkle when she works. In the evening, when she is free, she tells us stories about her village.

3. <u>Harry Potter -the wizard</u>

Harry had always been small and skinny for his age. He looked even smaller and skinnier when he wore old clothes of Dudley. Harry had a thin face, knobbly knees, black hair and bright green eyes. He wore round glasses held together with a lot of Sello-tape. The only thing Harry liked about his own appearance was very thin scar on his fore-head which was shaped like a bolt of lightning.

CHAPTER 12

SAID IS DEAD

"Said is Dead" is a concept that encourages students to avoid using the word "said" repetitively in their writing. By substituting it with more expressive and specific dialogue tags, students can enhance their writing and make it more engaging for readers. This practice helps students develop a wider vocabulary and improves their overall writing skills.

Instead of using "said" repeatedly, students can incorporate alternative dialogue tags that reflect the emotions, tone, or actions of the speaker. For example, instead of writing "John said," students can use tags such as "John exclaimed," "John whispered," "John shouted," or "John asked," depending on the context and the desired effect.

By diversifying the dialogue tags, students can bring their characters to life, create a more vivid narrative, and enhance the reader's experience. However, it is important to use these alternative tags sparingly and only when they are appropriate and contribute to the understanding of the story.

Sample Text:

Paragraph: Sophie and Mark were browsing through a bookstore, looking for their next read. "This book seems interesting," remarked Sophie. "Let me read the back cover," suggested Mark. "It's a mystery novel," observed Sophie. "I enjoy thrilling stories," stated Mark. "Shall we buy it?" asked Sophie. "Yes, let's add it to our collection," agreed Mark. "We can also check out the fantasy section," suggested Sophie.

"Good idea, I love immersing myself in magical worlds," admitted Mark. "We'll have a fantastic time exploring these books," anticipated Sophie. "Absolutely," confirmed Mark, eager to continue their book adventure.

Look at this…..

Once upon a time, in a land not too far away, a group of animals gathered for a grand adventure. There was Simon the squirrel, Emma the elephant, Oliver the owl, and Rosie the rabbit. They were on a mission to find the lost treasure of Sparkle Island.

As they ventured deeper into the enchanted forest, they encountered a talking tree. The tree's name was Wise Willow, known for its vast knowledge and clever words.

"Hello, travellers," Wise Willow boomed with a wise smile. "Welcome to my humble abode. How can I assist you on your quest?"

"We seek the treasure of Sparkle Island," Simon chirped excitedly.

"Ah, the legendary treasure!" exclaimed Wise Willow, nodding sagely. "Well, my fine friends, I have some valuable advice for you."

Emma, being the curious elephant, trumpeted, "Please, Wise Willow, do share your wisdom."

Wise Willow chuckled softly and replied, "Of course, my dear Emma.

Remember, when you're telling your adventurous tale, it's important to make your characters' voices come alive. Instead of simply saying 'said,' you can use more descriptive words to show how they're speaking."

Oliver, the wise owl, hooted in agreement. "Indeed, let's embark on a linguistic adventure! What words could we use to replace 'said'?"

Rosie, the quick-witted rabbit, piped up, "How about 'exclaimed' for when we're excited? Like this: 'We found the treasure!' exclaimed Simon."

Simon nodded and added, "And when we're asking questions, we can say 'inquired.' For example, 'Where is the treasure hidden?' inquired Emma."

Emma's ears perked up, and she added, "When we're feeling scared, we can use 'whispered.' So, if we're frightened, we could say, 'I think there's something spooky here,' whispered Rosie."

Wise Willow beamed with delight. "Wonderful suggestions, my adventurous friends!

By using expressive words like these, your story will come alive with vivid characters and emotions."

The animal adventurers exchanged excited glances, ready to embark on their treasure hunt armed with a new understanding of how to bring their tale to life.

In this extract, the concept of "Said Is Dead" is introduced as a way to enhance storytelling. The characters in the story suggest alternative words like "exclaimed," "inquired," and "whispered" to replace the word "said." This encourages children to be creative and use descriptive language to convey the emotions and manner of speaking of the characters in their own stories.

12.1 Banks:

The emotion of ANGER				
accused	argued	badgered	barked	bellowed
bickered	chastised	chided	commanded	complained
corrected	countered	cursed	demanded	denounced
disagreed	exploded	fumed	growled	grumbled
harshly	hissed	hollered	howled	huffed
interrupted	muttered	objected	ordered	raged
ranted	retaliated	retorted	roared	scoffed
scolded	scowled	screamed	screeched	seethed

shot	shouted	shrilled	snapped	snarled
sneered	stormed	swore	taunted	threatened
warned	yelled			

The action of ANSWERING				
acknowledged	added	answered	articulated	clarified
commented	conceded	concurred	deflected	disputed
explained	interjected	protested	reassured	remarked
replied	responded	stated		

The emotion of DISGUST				
cringed	groused	grunted	mocked	rasped
refused	sniffed	snorted		

The emotion of EMBARRASSMENT				
admitted	confessed	hesitated	mumbled	sheepishly
spluttered				

The emotion of FEAR				
babbled	croaked	denied	doubted	fretted
groaned	gulped	moaned	panted	prayed
quavered	shrieked	slurred	squeaked	squealed
stammered	stuttered	whimpered	whined	whispered
worried				

The emotion of HAPPINESS				
approved	beamed	bubbled	burst	cackled
chatted	chattered	cheered	chirped	chortled
chorused	chuckled	complimented	congratulated	cooed
crowed	effused	exulted	forgave	giggled
grinned	gurgled	gushed	hummed	joked
praised	resounded	sang	simpered	smiled
Squealed	thanked	whooped		

Words associated with PERSUATION 😊				
advised	appealed	asserted	assured	avowed
begged	beseeched	cajoled	claimed	convinced
directed	encouraged	entreated	implored	needled
pleaded	stressed	suggested	urged	

Words associated with PROVOCATION 😈				
bragged	dared	exasperated	gibed	goaded
insulted	jested	jeered	joked	lied
mimicked	nagged	provoked	quipped	sassed
smirked	snickered			

The emotion of SADNESS 😢				
apologized	bawled	bewailed	blubbered	comforted
consoled	cried	glumly	lamented	mumbled
mumbled	murmured	sighed	sniffled	sobbed
spilled	wailed	wept		

The emotion of SURPRISE 😮				
bleated	blurted	exclaimed	gasped	marveled
perplexed	sputtered	yelped		

Words associated with QUESTIONS or CURIOSITY 🤔				
asked	challenged	coaxed	hinted	inquired
pleaded	puzzled	queried	questioned	quizzed
wondered				

Words associated with UNCERTAINTY or CONFUSION 😕				
cautioned	doubtfully	guessed	hesitated	vacillated

The emotion of LOVE or Romance 💕				
breathed	expressed	flirted	flirtatiously	proclaimed
promised	purred	swooned		

Words associated with TIREDNESS 😫				
feebly	groggily	lethargically	listlessly	sleepily
somnolently	wearily	yawned		
Words not associated with any particular emotion 🌀				
acquiesced	added	addressed	affirmed	agreed
alliterated	announced	aside	began	bet
boasted	boomed	called	chimed in	coached
concluded	confided	confirmed	considered	continued
contributed	conversed	deadpanned	decided	declared
defended	demurred	described	disclosed	divulged
drawled	echoed	emphasized	ended	faltered
finished	gloated	greeted	heaved	hypothesized
imitated	implied	informed	insinuated	insisted
intoned	instructed	jabbered	lectured	maintained
mentioned	monotoned	motioned	mouthed	mused
nodded	noted	notified	observed	offered
opined	peeped	peppered	pestered	piped
pointed out	pondered	prattled	pressed	pronounced
proposed	put in	quietly	quoted	rambled
rattled on	read	reasoned	recalled	reckoned
recited	recounted	reiterated	related	remembered
reminded	repeated	reported	requested	restated
revealed	rhymed	ridiculed	sibilated	sneezed
snickered	speculated	spoke	started	surmised
sympathized	tartly	teased	tempted	tested
testified	theorized	thought aloud	told	trilled
uttered	ventured	verified	volunteered	vowed
went on	wheezed	wished	yakked	yapped
wheezed	wished	yakked	yapped	yawned

12.2 Sample Worksheets:

1. Read the following extract and replace 'Said' with appropriate words. Refer to your handbook.

'The Big Friendly Giant makes his magic powders out of the dreams that children dream when they are asleep', he said.

'How?' I said. 'Tell me how, Dad.'

'Ah', my father said. ' That is the interesting part'.

'The BFG can hear the dreams', he said.

'What happens when he catches the dreams?' I said.

'He imprisons them in glass bottles',my father said.

'The BfG always carries a suitcase and a blow pipe',my father said.

'More about it tomorrow. Good night Danny. Go to sleep', said father.

2. Replace the word "said" with a more expressive and specific dialogue tag.

Write your revised sentence in the space provided.

Example: Sentence: "I'm so excited," she said. Revised sentence: "I'm so excited," she exclaimed.

Worksheet:

"I can't believe it," he _______________.

"Be careful," she _______________.

"I don't understand," he _______________.

"Let's go!" they _______________.

"What a surprise," she _______________.

"Please stop," he _______________.

"I'm sorry," she _______________.

"That's incredible," he _______________.

"What do you mean?" she _______________.

"I'm really tired," he _______________.

CHAPTER 13

NARRATIVE ESSAY

13.1 Introduction:

A narrative essay is a type of writing that tells a story or shares a personal experience from the perspective of the author/narrator. It typically includes characters, a plot, and a vivid description of events or experiences to engage the reader's senses and emotions.

When writing a narrative essay, one might think of it as telling a story. These essays are often anecdotal, experiential, and personal—allowing students to express themselves in a creative and, quite often, moving ways.

- Narrates a story, incident or an event. It focuses on actions and sequence of action (chronological order).
- Often it is first person point of view I and me.
- It tells about the character (action and speech), location (place and details), their actions in the order of occurrence.
- Add all WH and HOW.
- Use Descriptive vocabulary: use adjectives, verbs, adverbs, idioms, figurative language.
- e. g. Events, incidents, accidents, festivals, functions, journey, natural disaster etc.

13.2 Format:

I. Introduction

  ➢ Start with a hook to grab the reader's attention, such as an interesting fact, a quote, or a rhetorical question.

> Provide a brief overview of the topic or the event you will be discussing in the essay.

> State the thesis statement, which should clearly express the main idea or the purpose of the essay.

II. Body Paragraphs

> Develop the story or experience in chronological order, using descriptive language and sensory details to create a vivid image in the reader's mind.

> Use dialogue, if applicable, to make the story more engaging and authentic.

> Show, don't tell. Use specific examples and anecdotes to illustrate the events and emotions of the story.

> Include reflections or insights that show the significance of the story or the experience to the author.

> Use transitions to smoothly connect ideas and events.

III. Conclusion

> Summarize the main points or events of the story.

> Restate the thesis statement in a different way.

> Provide a closing statement that leaves a lasting impression on the reader.

> Tell about the lesson learnt from the experience.

Narrative Essay Format:

> **Title:** A descriptive and engaging title that reflects the essence of the story.

> **Introduction:** Hook, brief overview, thesis statement.

> **Body Paragraphs**: Develop the story or experience with vivid details, dialogue, and reflections.

> **Conclusion:** Summarize main points, restate thesis statement, provide a closing statement. Move to present focussing on what you learnt from the event.

NARRATIVE WRITING

Re-telling a incident or event

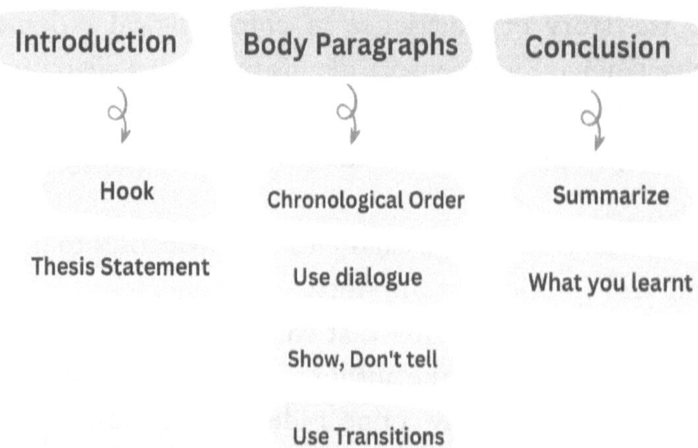

FEATURES OF NARRATIVE WRITING

Good narrative writing has the following features.

- It begins with a **good introduction.**
- The narrative is built around a **theme** or themes.
- **Characters** and **locales** are created skilfully.
- **Chronological** or **dramatic sequence** is used.
- It provides a situation of **conflict,** or complication or problem.
- It works up to a **resolution.**
- It has an effective **ending.**
- Characters show **growth** in the story.
- The **past tense** is generally used in narration.
- The first or the third person narrative **point-of-view** is used.
- **Dialogues** help to break the monotony of narration and make it interesting.

13.3 Sample Essay

A Visit to an Amusement Park

It was a sunny Saturday morning when my family and I decided to embark on this thrilling adventure.

As we arrived at the park, a vibrant world of colours and sounds welcomed us. The air was filled with laughter, screams of excitement, and the joyful melodies of carnival music. The sight before us was awe-inspiring. Towering roller coasters reached for the sky, spinning rides twirled gracefully, and children ran around with wide smiles on their faces.

Our first stop was the Ferris wheel, standing tall and majestic against the clear blue sky. I felt a mix of anticipation and nervousness as I boarded the gondola. As we ascended, the breath-taking view unfolded before my eyes. From the top, I could see the entire park, bustling with people and buzzing with activity. It was like a miniature city filled with happiness and joy.

Next, we made our way to the roller coasters, the heart-pounding kings of the park. The line seemed never-ending, but the excitement was contagious. The moment I stepped into the coaster car; my heart raced with anticipation. The ride began, and I could feel the rush of wind against my face as we zoomed through twists, turns, and loops. The adrenaline coursed through my veins, and I couldn't help but let out exhilarated screams. It was an adrenaline-fueled adventure like no other.

After experiencing the thrills of the roller coasters, we decided to explore the water rides. We eagerly hopped on a log flume ride, equipped with a steep drop and a splash landing. The anticipation built up as we slowly ascended to the top, our log bobbing up and down. Suddenly, we plummeted down the steep slope, and a tidal wave of water crashed over us, leaving us drenched but laughing uncontrollably. It was a refreshing break from the summer heat.

As the day progressed, we explored other attractions such as the spinning teacups, the bumper cars, and a lively circus performance. Everywhere we went, the atmosphere was filled with an infectious energy and a sense of adventure. We indulged in cotton candy, popcorn, and other delectable treats that added to the carnival ambiance.

As the sun began to set, the amusement park transformed into a magical wonderland. A kaleidoscope of colourful lights illuminated the rides and created a captivating spectacle. The laughter and excitement grew louder, as if the park had come alive with its own vibrant personality.

With heavy hearts, we bid farewell to the amusement park, but our memories would last forever. As I sat in the car on the way back home, I couldn't help but feel a sense of gratitude for the unforgettable experiences and the precious time spent with my loved ones.

Visiting the amusement park was like stepping into an area of pure joy and adventure. The sights, sounds, and sensations were beyond anything I had ever experienced. It was a day filled with laughter, thrills, and magical moments that I will treasure for a lifetime.

13.4 Sample Narrative essay

"Conquering the Mountain: Overcoming a Personal Challenge"

Last summer, I embarked on a solo hiking trip to the mountains, eager to test my physical and mental limits. Little did I know that this adventure would turn into one of the most challenging experiences of my life, pushing me to my limits and teaching me invaluable life lessons.

As I set off on the trailhead, I met an experienced hiker named Mark, who had been hiking the same trail. Mark had a calm and confident demeanour and offered to join me on my journey. I gladly accepted his company, hoping that his experience would be a valuable asset.

As we hiked deeper into the wilderness, the trail became steeper, the air thinner, and the weather more unpredictable. At one point, we encountered a narrow ridge with a sheer drop on one side and a daunting cliff on the other. Fear gripped me as I realized the magnitude of the challenge ahead. My knees trembled, my heart pounded, and my mind raced with self-doubt.

Mark noticed my unease and came up to me, putting a reassuring hand on my shoulder. "Don't worry, you've got this," he said with a confident smile. "Just take it one step at a time and focus on your footing. I'll be right beside you."

His words and presence gave me the boost of confidence I needed. I took a deep breath, gathered my courage, and followed his lead. We carefully navigated the ridge, one step at a time, encouraging each other along the way.

As we moved forward, the weather worsened, with rain and fog reducing visibility. The trail became slippery and treacherous, and our progress slowed down. Mark took out his rain gear and offered me some extra supplies to ensure we were well-prepared. He also shared stories of his past hiking adventures, distracting me from the challenges at hand and helping me stay focused.

As we ascended higher, the altitude took a toll on my body. I struggled to catch my breath, and every step felt like an uphill battle. Doubt and exhaustion threatened to overwhelm me, but Mark remained by my side, offering words of encouragement and reminding me to take breaks and stay hydrated.

After what seemed like an eternity, we finally reached the summit. The feeling of accomplishment and triumph was indescribable. We stood at the peak, surrounded by breath-taking views of the mountains, valleys, and clouds below.

I turned to Mark, tears of gratitude in my eyes. "I couldn't have done it without you," I said, my voice choked with emotion. "Thank you for believing in me and pushing me to keep going."

Mark smiled and clapped me on the back. "You did it all on your own," he said. "I was just here to lend a helping hand. You showed incredible determination and resilience. I'm proud of you."

The journey back down was not easy either, but with Mark's guidance and support, I felt a newfound confidence and strength. I learned the importance of companionship, of having someone by your side during challenging times, and the power of believing in oneself.

As we descended the mountain and reached the base, I felt a sense of accomplishment and gratitude that words could not express. The challenge had tested my physical and mental limits, but it had also brought me a newfound friendship and valuable life lessons.

In the end, facing the challenge of hiking a mountain had been a defining experience in my life. It had pushed me to my limits, but it had also revealed the importance of companionship, perseverance, and self-belief. It had taught me that challenges are opportunities for growth, and that with determination, courage, and the support of others, we can overcome any obstacle that comes our way.

Note:

Always remember to revise and edit the essay to suit your own writing style and voice, and make sure to check for grammar, punctuation, and coherence. Personalize the essay with your own experiences and emotions to make it authentic and genuine.

13.5 Lesson Plan:

Objective: By the end of this lesson, students will be able to:

> Understand the basic structure and elements of a narrative essay.
> Identify the key components of a compelling narrative.
> Write a well-structured narrative essay.

Materials Needed:

> Whiteboard and markers or a digital board
> Handouts or digital copies of narrative essay samples
> Laptops or paper and pens for students

Introduction:

Begin the lesson by discussing what a narrative essay is. Define it as a form of writing that tells a story, typically in the first person, and shares personal experiences, anecdotes, or events.

Explain the importance of narrative essays, such as their ability to engage readers, convey a message, or provide insight into the writer's experiences.

Main Content:

Step 1: The Structure of a Narrative Essay

> Discuss the basic structure of a narrative essay:
> Introduction: Set the scene, introduce the characters, and provide context.
> Body: Develop the plot, characters, and events. Use descriptive language and dialogue. Create Rising Action.
> Conclusion: Reflect on the experience, share the lesson learned, or provide closure.
> Emphasize the importance of a clear beginning, middle, and end in narrative essays.

Step 2: Key Elements of a Narrative

Discuss the essential elements of a compelling narrative:

➢ Characters: Who are the central characters in the story?
➢ Setting: Where and when does the story take place?
➢ Conflict: What challenges or problems do the characters face?
➢ Plot: What is the sequence of events in the story?
➢ Resolution: How is the conflict resolved or what is the outcome?
➢ Theme: What is the central message or lesson of the narrative?
➢ Provide examples to illustrate each element.

Step 3: Writing a Narrative Essay

➢ Introduce the writing process for a narrative essay:
➢ Brainstorming: Generate ideas for potential topics or experiences to write about.
➢ Outlining: Create a rough outline of the introduction, body paragraphs, and conclusion.
➢ Drafting: Write the essay, focusing on vivid descriptions and engaging storytelling.
➢ Revising and Editing: Review and refine the essay for clarity, coherence, and grammar.
➢ Provide tips on how to hook the reader in the introduction and conclude the essay effectively.

Activity:

➢ Divide students into pairs or small groups.
➢ Provide each group with a sample narrative essay.
➢ Instruct students to analyse the essay and identify its key elements, structure, and any particularly engaging storytelling techniques.
➢ After analysing the samples, have each group share their findings with the class.
➢ Finally, give them a prompt to work on and write their essays and share it with the class.

Conclusion:

> ➤ Summarize the key points covered in the lesson, emphasizing the structure and elements of a narrative essay.
> ➤ Encourage students to start brainstorming topics for their own narrative essays.
> ➤ Assign homework, if applicable, which may include selecting a topic and beginning the brainstorming process for their narrative essays.

13.6 Induction activities we can take to introduce Narrative writing

Induction activities are essential to engage students and introduce them to narrative writing effectively. These activities should be fun, interactive, and designed to pique students' interest in the topic.

Here are some induction activities you can use:

1. **Storytelling Circle**: Have students sit in a circle, and start by sharing a brief personal anecdote or story. Encourage each student to take turns sharing a short story or anecdote from their own lives. This can help them get comfortable with sharing personal experiences, a crucial aspect of narrative writing.

2. **Picture Prompts**: Show students a series of interesting or evocative images. Ask them to select one image and write a short paragraph or a few sentences about what they see in the picture. This can stimulate their creativity and provide material for future narrative essays.

3. **Story Starters:** Provide students with a list of interesting story starters or opening lines. Ask them to choose one and continue the story for a few minutes. This activity can help students practice beginning a narrative in an engaging way.

4. **Reading Aloud**: Start the class by reading a short, engaging narrative excerpt aloud. Afterward, facilitate a discussion about

what made the passage interesting and compelling. This activity can help students identify effective narrative techniques.

5. **Storytelling Game**: Play a storytelling game where each student adds one sentence to a growing narrative. Start with a simple prompt, such as "Once upon a time, in a mysterious forest..." and go around the room, with each student adding to the story. This collaborative activity encourages creativity and cooperation.

6. **Music and Mood**: Play a piece of instrumental music that evokes a particular mood (e.g., happiness, sadness, excitement). Ask students to write a short paragraph or story inspired by the mood of the music. This activity helps them understand the role of mood and atmosphere in narrative writing.

7. **Analysing a Short Story**: Provide students with a short story to read, and then discuss it as a class. Focus on elements like character development, plot structure, and the use of descriptive language. This can serve as an introduction to narrative elements.

8. **Comparing Genres**: Show students examples of different types of writing (e.g., news article, poem, narrative essay). Discuss the characteristics that make each type unique, and then introduce narrative writing as a distinct genre.

Remember to adapt these activities to the age and proficiency level of your students, and encourage open discussion and sharing of ideas throughout the induction process. These activities should set a positive and engaging tone for the narrative writing unit.

Use of Transitional Words:

Use this as a sample text to explain Linkers

Yesterday, I went on a hike in the mountains. Firstly, I packed a backpack with water, snacks, and sunscreen. Next, I drove to the trailhead and parked my car. Then, I put on my hiking boots and started walking up the trail. As I climbed higher, the air became cooler and the views became more breathtaking. After a few hours of hiking, I reached the summit and sat down to take in the view. Finally, I started the descent back down the mountain, feeling exhausted but exhilarated by my accomplishment.

Transition Words and Phrases in English

Emphasis	Opinion	Addition	illustration
Significantly	I think	In addition	For example
Notably	I believe	Further	Such as
In particular	I feel	Furthermore	For instance
In fact	In my opinion	Besides	Such as
Actually	In my view	In addition to	In other words
	As far as I know	Moreover	An instance
	It seems likely	Additionally	As revealed by
	It seems to me	Not only … but also	To show that
		Then	In the case of
		Again	As an example
		Finally	For one thing
Persuasion	**Contrast**	**Conclusion**	**Cause & Effect**
Of course	However	To conclude	Since
Clearly	Nevertheless	In conclusion	For
Evidently	Alternatively	Finally	So
Surely	Despite this	On the whole	Consequently
Indeed	On the contrary	Summarising	Therefore
Undoubtedly	Yet	Overall	Thus
Decidedly	Whereas	To sum up	Hence
Certainly	Apart from	Evidently	Owing to
For this reason	Even so		As a result of
Besides	Although		Causes
Again	In spite of		As a consequence of
	While		

Comparison

Equally

As with

Likewise

In the same way

Similarly

Like

Of contrast

Despite this

In comparison

In contrast

Even though

13.7 Question Bank-

1. Write an account about an occasion when you were put in charge of looking after your younger siblings in the absence of your parents and how you handled them.

2. Narrate your experience as a volunteer at a free primary school in your locality.

3. Write about a memorable day in your life as head Girl/Head Boy of your school

4. Narrate frightening experience that you had in past.

5. Write about a class project that you planned and executed along with your classmates.

6. Write about how your friendship with your closest friend began.

7. Narrate an experience that you went through when you misjudged someone and then realized your fault.

8. Narrate a humorous account of a series of comic incidents that occurred due a power cut.

9. Write about the first time you received a prize for an achievement.

10. Your success in something after a lot of hard work

11. Write an essay about your favourite teacher in school, narrating how and why she/he became your favourite. Also mention the change she/he has inspired in you.

12. Write an essay on an activity, such as swimming or playing a musical instrument, that you have grown to love from the time when you first started learning it.

13. Write an essay about your failure in something and how that incident inspired you to work harder.

14. Write a narrative essay on a story your parents/grandparents have told you and what you learnt from it.

15. Write an essay narrating an incident or anecdote involving your best friend.

16. The moment you met someone who changed your life

17. Something embarrassing that happened to you

18. A random act of kindness

19. The end of long cherished friendship

20. Write about a time when you faced a challenge and how you overcame it.

21. Share a personal story of a meaningful encounter with a stranger.

22. Write about a travel adventure that changed your perspective on life.

23. Narrate an experience that you went through when you misjudged someone and then realized your fault.

24. Narrate a humorous account of a series of comic incidents that occurred due a power cut.

25. Imagine receiving a mysterious package in the mail. Write a narrative about what happens when you open it and the unexpected journey it takes you on.

26. The Haunted House: Write a narrative about a spooky encounter in a haunted house. Describe the eerie atmosphere, the mysterious occurrences, and how you bravely faced your fears.

27. Share about a fear you had and how you overcame it. Describe the fear, what steps you took to face it, and how you felt once you conquered it.

13.8 Sample Worksheets:

The trip I enjoyed the most

The day I won the Competition

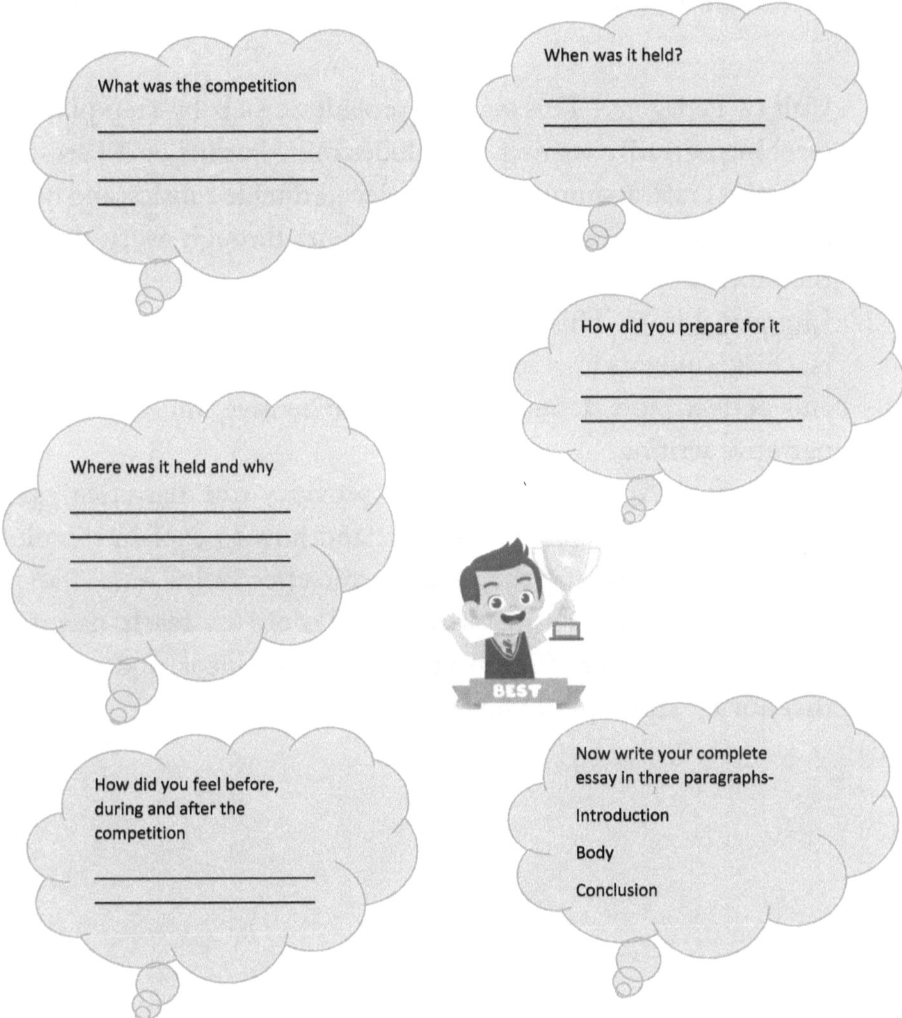

Sample Literature References: to be put

13.9 Links for reference:

Here are some websites that can help you with teaching narrative essay writing:

1. <u>Cult of Pedagogy:</u> This website provides a step-by-step plan for teaching narrative writing. It includes mini-lessons on 14 areas of narrative craft, a sample narrative piece, editable rubrics, and other supplemental materials to guide students through every stage of the process.

2. <u>Literacy Ideas:</u> This website offers a complete solution to teaching students how to craft creative characters, superb settings, and perfect plots. It includes a comprehensive unit on teaching narrative writing.

3. <u>My Perfect Words:</u> This website provides free narrative essay examples that can help you understand how to explain the plot, characters, setting, and the entire theme effectively.

4. <u>wiki How:</u> This website provides 14 steps to teach narrative writing. It includes assigning model essays, videos, and podcasts that are age-appropriate for your students.

CHAPTER 14

IMAGINATIVE ESSAY

14.1 Introduction

An "imaginative essay" is a type of creative writing that uses the writer's imagination to create a story or a narrative.

This type of essay allows the writer to use creative techniques such as descriptive language, symbolism, and figurative language to make the story come alive. The goal of an imaginative essay is to entertain, engage the reader's emotions, and provide a unique perspective on the topic.

Imaginative essays can be written in different forms, such as a short story, a descriptive piece, or a personal reflection. In an imaginative essay, the writer has the freedom to create a narrative that is not limited by facts or evidence, but it should be consistent and believable.

The main characteristic of an imaginative essay is that it is written with the purpose of entertaining, allowing the reader to escape reality for a moment and to immerse in the world created by the writer. It is a form of creative writing that can be used in literature, poetry, and other forms of writing as well.

Imaginative essays challenge students to stretch their creative muscles and think critically. These essays encourage students to express their unique ideas, emotions, and perspectives, fostering a deeper connection with the written word.

14.2 Format of Imaginative Essay.

Imaginative essays follow a structured format to engage readers and convey vivid stories or ideas effectively.

1. Introduction

The introduction should grab the reader's attention with a compelling hook.

Include a clear thesis statement that previews the essay's main idea or theme.

2. Body Paragraphs

Organize the body paragraphs logically, each containing a single idea or event.

Use descriptive language, vivid imagery, and literary devices to engage the reader.

Show, don't tell: Encourage students to create mental pictures through their writing.

3. Conclusion

Summarize the main points and restate the thesis statement.

End with a thought-provoking or memorable closing statement.

14.3 Sample Imaginative Essay

To illustrate the concepts discussed, let's explore a sample imaginative essay titled "The Enchanted Forest." This essay showcases effective techniques and engages readers with imaginative storytelling.

<u>The Day I Discovered My Superpower</u>

Have you ever dreamed of having a superpower? Well, I used to dream about it all the time. I thought it would be fantastic to fly like a bird or have the strength of a superhero. Little did I know that one day, my dream would come true.

It was a warm summer afternoon, and I was playing in the park with my friends. We decided to have a picnic under a big, old oak tree. As we munched on sandwiches and chips, something incredible happened.

I was reaching for a bag of potato chips when I accidentally knocked it out of my friend's hand. The bag flew through the air, and I watched in amazement as it floated, suspended in mid-air, just inches away from my face. My friends stared wide-eyed, and I could hardly believe what I was seeing.

One particular incident that stood out was when I saw a little girl crying because her favourite red balloon had drifted too high for her to reach. Tears streamed down her face as she pointed to the balloon, floating just out of her reach. Without thinking, I focused my mind on the balloon and gently brought it down into her waiting hands. The little girl's face lit up with joy, and her smile was brighter than the sun. It was a moment I would never forget.

After that incredible balloon rescue, I realized that I was the one who had made it happen. I tried to move it around with my hand, and to my astonishment, it followed my every command. I had telekinesis – the power to move things with my mind!

My friends and I spent the rest of the day experimenting with my newfound ability. We made leaves dance in the air, pushed swings higher and faster, and even stacked rocks with our minds. It was the most incredible day of my life.

As the sun began to set, we gathered around the picnic blanket and talked about how amazing it was to have superpowers, even if just for a day. We promised to keep my secret safe, knowing that having a superpower came with great responsibility.

That night, I lay in bed, still in awe of what had happened. I realized that having a superpower wasn't just about flying or having super strength. It was about using that power to help others and make the world a better place.

The next day, I went to the park with a new purpose. I used my telekinesis to help people – picking up litter, rescuing kites stuck in trees, and even helping a lost puppy find its way home. It felt incredible to make a difference in the world, even if it was in a small way.

As the days turned into weeks, my superpower became a part of who I was. I continued to use it for good, and it brought me closer to my friends, who were always there to support me. I learned that having a superpower wasn't just about the abilities you had; it was about the choices you made.

So, the next time you find yourself daydreaming about having a superpower, remember that you might already have one inside you. It might not be the power to fly or become invisible, but it could be something even more incredible – the power to make a positive impact on the world and the lives of those around you.

And who knows, maybe one day you'll discover your own superpower, just like I did on that warm summer afternoon under the old oak tree.

Analysis

Break down the essay, highlighting the use of hooks, thesis statements, descriptive language, and literary devices.

14.4 Topics/Prompts for Imaginative Essay

1. Write an Imaginative Essay – 'Imagine you were a character in a novel and describe your journey.'
2. Write an Imaginative Essay – Imagine you were a superhero and describe your powers and how you use them

3. Write an Imaginative Essay – Imagine you were living in a different era and describe your daily life

4. Write an Imaginative Essay – If you were a traveller to a different planet and what would be your experience

5. Write an Imaginative Essay – Imagine you were a detective and describe solving a mystery

6. Write an Imaginative Essay – Imagine you are a ghost and describe your afterlife

7. Imagine you were a robot and describe your programming and purpose

8. Imagine you were a time traveller and describe your journey through history

9. Imagine you were a genie and describe your life in a lamp

   If you got trapped in the mall overnight, what would you do there? Describe all the fun hijinks you could have.

   Write a fake news story about something real that happened this week.

   If trees could talk, what sorts of things would they have to say?

   Write a sequel to your favourite fairy tale.

10. Imagine that you found a map to a hidden treasure. Narrate a story on how you would reach to the treasure.

CHAPTER 15

DISCURSIVE WRITING/PERSUASIVE WRITING/ARGUMENTATIVE WRITING

Persuasive	Argumentative
Appeals to Emotions	Appeals to Logic
May make a claim based on opinions	Makes claim based of facts and evidence
Evidences can be anecdotal or based on personal experiences	Evidences based on research studies, statistics and experts opinions
Subjective and emotive tone	Objective and Formal tone

15.1 Introduction

Persuasive writing and Argumentative essay writing are both forms of essay writing that aim to convince the reader of a particular viewpoint or argument.

While they have some similarities, there are a few key differences between the two.

1. Purpose: The primary purpose of persuasive writing is to persuade or influence the reader's opinion or behaviour. It often appeals to emotions, values, or beliefs to sway the audience.

2. On the other hand, argumentative essay writing focuses on presenting logical arguments supported by evidence to support a specific claim or position.

3. Tone: Persuasive writing tends to use a more subjective and emotive tone, employing techniques such as rhetorical questions, vivid language, and appeals to the reader's emotions.

   Argumentative essay writing, however, follows a more objective and formal tone, relying on logical reasoning, evidence, and counterarguments to support the claims made.

➢ Structure: In persuasive writing, the structure can be more flexible and creative. It often includes elements such as anecdotes, storytelling, or personal experiences to engage the reader.

   On the other hand, argumentative essays generally follow a structured format with an introduction that presents the thesis statement, body paragraphs that present evidence and arguments, and a conclusion that summarizes the main points and reinforces the thesis.

➢ Use of Evidence: Both persuasive writing and argumentative essays use evidence to support their claims, but the emphasis and type of evidence may differ.

   In persuasive writing, evidence can be anecdotal, emotional, or based on personal experiences.

   Argumentative essays, however, rely more on empirical evidence, research studies, statistics, and expert opinions to provide logical support for the arguments.

➢ Audience: Persuasive writing often aims to appeal to a broader audience, including those who may not have a deep understanding of the topic. It may use language and techniques to captivate a wide range of readers.

Argumentative essays, on the other hand, are typically written for a more academic or knowledgeable audience who expects a well-structured and evidence-based argument.

While these differences exist, it's important to note that persuasive writing and argumentative essays share the common goal of convincing the reader. The specific approach taken will depend on the purpose, context, and requirements of the writing task.

15.2 Sample Essays

Persuasive Essay:

Junk Food vs. Healthy Food

Introduction:

Imagine a world where everyone had the power to make healthier choices, resulting in a society full of vitality and well-being. This can become a reality if we start reevaluating our eating habits and opt for healthy food instead of succumbing to the temptations of junk food. While junk food may offer convenience and temporary satisfaction, it comes at a high price - our long-term health. By choosing healthy food, we can nourish our bodies, improve our overall well-being, and set a positive example for future generations.

Body Paragraphs:

Junk food may offer an array of mouthwatering flavours and textures, but healthy food can be equally delicious. With some creativity and culinary exploration, we can discover a vast range of healthy and nutritious options that tickle our taste buds. Fruits, vegetables, whole grains, lean proteins, and plant-based alternatives provide an abundance of flavours, and when prepared skilfully, they can rival any junk food indulgence.

One of the key differences between junk food and healthy food lies in their nutritional value. While junk food is often high in unhealthy fats, sugar, and sodium, healthy food provides essential nutrients, vitamins, and minerals that fuel our bodies. Whole foods like fruits, vegetables, nuts, and lean proteins offer a wide spectrum of nutrients, promoting physical and mental well-being. By choosing healthy food, we give our bodies the nourishment they need to thrive.

Indulging in junk food regularly can have detrimental effects on our health. Obesity, heart disease, diabetes, and other chronic illnesses are often associated with a diet rich in unhealthy food choices. On the contrary, a diet rich in healthy food can help prevent such diseases and promote longevity. By making conscious choices and prioritizing our health, we can significantly reduce the risk of these health conditions and enjoy a better quality of life.

Environmental Impact:

Beyond personal health, our food choices also impact the environment. The production of junk food often involves excessive use of resources, contributes to deforestation, and generates significant greenhouse gas emissions.

On the other hand, healthy food options such as locally sourced fruits and vegetables, organic products, and plant-based alternatives have a lower environmental footprint. By choosing healthy food, we support sustainable practices and contribute to a healthier planet.

Conclusion:

In the battle between junk food and healthy food, the choice is clear. While junk food may provide temporary pleasure, it comes at the cost of long-term health consequences. Opting for healthy food allows us to nourish our bodies, maintain overall well-being, and promote a sustainable future. By making conscious choices today, we can create a healthier society and inspire others to join us on this journey towards a brighter and more vibrant future.

Argumentative Essay:

Junk Food vs. Healthy Food

Introduction:

The debate between junk food and healthy food has been ongoing, with advocates on both sides passionately defending their viewpoints. While some argue that junk food provides convenience and indulgence, others emphasize the importance of healthy food for long-term well-being. By examining the nutritional value, health effects, and environmental impact, it becomes evident that healthy food is the superior choice for individuals and society as a whole.

Body Paragraphs:

Healthy food offers a broad range of nutrients essential for our bodies' optimal functioning. Fruits, vegetables, whole grains, lean proteins, and dairy products provide vitamins, minerals, antioxidants, and dietary fibre necessary for maintaining good health. On the other hand, junk food is often high in unhealthy fats, added sugars, and sodium, lacking the essential nutrients required for a balanced diet. Choosing healthy food ensures that we meet our nutritional needs and support overall well-being.

Regular consumption of junk food has been linked to numerous health issues, including obesity, cardiovascular diseases, diabetes, and certain types of cancer. The excessive intake of processed food, sugary beverages, and snacks laden with trans fats contributes to the rising prevalence of these conditions. Conversely, adopting a diet rich in healthy food reduces the risk of chronic illnesses and promotes longevity. The evidence overwhelmingly supports the notion that healthy food choices are vital for maintaining good health.

The environmental consequences of our food choices are significant factors to consider. The production, processing, and packaging of junk food contribute to deforestation, excessive water usage, and greenhouse gas emissions. Conversely, healthy food options, such as locally sourced fruits and vegetables, organic farming practices, and plant-based alternatives, have a lower environmental footprint. By choosing healthy food, we can support sustainable agricultural practices and contribute to mitigating climate change.

An argument often raised against healthy food is its perceived higher cost and limited accessibility. However, investing in education and promoting initiatives that teach individuals about nutrition, cooking skills, and budget-friendly healthy options can help overcome these barriers. By fostering a culture that values and prioritizes health, we can make healthy food more accessible and affordable for all, ensuring that everyone has the opportunity to make informed dietary choices.

Conclusion:

When evaluating the arguments surrounding junk food and healthy food, the overwhelming evidence supports the superiority of healthy food for our overall well-being and the environment. With its nutritional value, positive health effects, and sustainability, healthy food emerges as the clear choice. By promoting education, improving accessibility, and emphasizing the long-term benefits, we can create a society that embraces healthy food as a fundamental pillar of a thriving and sustainable future.

15.3 AI- Boon or Bane

In a world of progress and development, we constantly work towards betterment. Throughout the years, change has been feared every time it comes. Yet the fear is proven wrong eventually. Truthfully put, the fears are understandable and not unnecessary. Although I stand with change and its viciously captivating nature. What I am discussing today is; the topic of AI. The most interesting and captivating/controversial topic of our time.

AI is necessarily artificial intelligence. A technology that has very recently broken the internet. It is what runs search engines, robots, softwares and now many other positions in the corporate industry. I stand with this change and believe it can do wonders in various industries.

The reason I so firmly believe that this will do us good is; firstly, it can take over many positions in the industry that are occupied by individuals who can do better in other fields where human touch is more necessary. For example, call centres/ customer care occupy hundreds of individuals who can instead work in industries of their own expertise. That can be fashion, food etc. This also encourages artists who resort to more conservative professions due to higher acceptance and need.

Next, AI simplifies work in corporate offices, this means more work get done in half the time. It also results in workers getting more time to themselves and being able to work from anywhere; while resting.

Thirdly, I would like to put forward he point that government work takes a lot of time in any country you go and technology can simplify many complicated procedures. Moreover, if AI takes over it, people can avoid travelling for hours and get it done at home. Need verification for visa, let AI send your application, scan it, and verify it before approving. This can prove a pivotal change in the lay man's life.

If you should point out, but oh, unemployment will starve us all. I believe, it cannot. As Narayan Murthy said 'AI will prove an excellent companion for all humans doing jobs.' People doing more analytical work can use AI to increase accuracy, those in industries like make up and cosmetics, can use it to help figure what will look good on clients. It will also fulfil the ever-lasting need of corporate industries and open up places for people in artistic areas that need human touch. Be it art or music, AI cannot do what humans do. This naturally creates more high paying opportunities in areas people avoid due to low pay rate.

In conclusion, I hope we will be able to advance with time and create an even safer place online with the help of such advanced technology. I expect this change, like every other, will surprise us for the better.

– By Janhavi Battalwar

Social Media

Social media plays a very important role and has influence in virtually every aspect of our lives. It is considered as the best source to know about the happenings of the world. Newspaper, magazine, radio, television and Internet are the different types of media. It greatly affects our lives because media has the power to influence our thoughts. This influence is sometimes positive and sometimes negative.

It is difficult to imagine the modern world without computers, information technology, and the Internet, because they have already had a special place in the life of each person. Social networks are very popular. We create accounts and visit our pages at least several times a week. This is an opportunity to communicate with family and friends who are away from us. Social networks provide an opportunity to communicate with colleagues at work, relatives and friends who live in different cities and countries, as well as make new acquaintances.

Social networks can be used as a tool for self-development. Here you can watch educational films, listen to good music, read interesting books and learn foreign languages. In social networks, interest groups have been created which you can find information of interest to you, for example, a video with fitness classes or with guitar lessons.

Along with this, social networks can help during the educational process. With their help, you can exchange lecture notes, assignments for laboratory work and other useful information. Also, there is the opportunity to join the community of certain subjects and study in detail questions on history or to tighten up knowledge of a foreign language. To do this, social networks have links to the necessary literature, photo and video materials; you can discuss problem issues with other members of the group.

Social networks are a platform for business development. Here you can advertise your online store, a web design studio or a music school. You can find new customers here and multiply the loyalty of regular customers.

However, as every coin has two sides, similarly, media has positive and negative effects.

Media is very influential for the people who resort to violence. Studies have suggested that the exposure to violence through television, movies and video games make children more aggressive, fearful, less trusting and more accepting of violence.

Some advertisements try to influence people by telling them the importance of branded items. As a result, children and youngsters become status conscious and start believing that by using these items they can create an image of high status in the society.

However, it is too early to draw final conclusions on this issue. Though it can be said that social networks have different impact on different people, depending on many conditions, and above all - on their personality traits.

15.4 Lesson Plan:

An effective induction activity for teaching argumentative and persuasive essays is a class debate. The debate allows students to actively engage with the topic, develop arguments, and practice persuasive speaking. Here's a step-by-step guide to conducting a debate as an induction activity:

- ➢ Topic Selection: Choose a debatable topic related to the subject matter or theme of the essays. Ensure it is broad enough to allow for multiple perspectives.

- ➢ Team Formation: Divide the class into two or more teams. Each team will represent a different viewpoint on the topic. Encourage students to take on roles such as team captain, researcher, or speaker.
- ➢ Research and Preparation: Allocate sufficient time for students to research their assigned position and gather supporting evidence. They should be encouraged to find credible sources and build well-rounded arguments.
- ➢ Argument Development: Instruct students to outline their arguments, identify key points, and anticipate counterarguments. Encourage critical thinking and analysis of their position.
- ➢ Rehearsal and Practice: Give students time to rehearse their arguments within their teams. This will help them refine their speaking skills and build confidence in presenting their viewpoints.
- ➢ Debate Format: Decide on the debate format, such as a structured formal debate with set time limits for each speaker, or a more casual panel discussion. Provide guidelines for respectful and constructive communication during the debate.
- ➢ Debate Session: Conduct the debate, allowing each team to present their arguments, provide evidence, and respond to counterarguments. Encourage active listening and respectful engagement from all participants.
- ➢ Reflection and Analysis: After the debate, facilitate a discussion where students reflect on the persuasive techniques used, strengths and weaknesses of arguments, and the impact of evidence on the overall persuasive effect.
- ➢ Essay Connection: Connect the debate experience to the structure and techniques used in persuasive essays. Discuss how the debate's arguments, evidence, and reasoning can be translated into written form.
- ➢ Individual Writing: Assign students to write their own argumentative or persuasive essays based on the debate topic or

a related topic. Provide guidelines and examples to support their writing process.

By incorporating a class debate as an induction activity, students will actively engage with the topic, practice persuasive speaking and critical thinking skills, and gain insights into constructing effective arguments for their essays.

CHAPTER 16

INFORMAL/PERSONAL LETTER WRITING

14.1 Introduction:

A personal letter is a type of letter written to a friend, family member, or loved one. It is typically written in an informal style and expresses the writer's thoughts, feelings, and experiences. Personal letters are often used to stay in touch with people who live far away, to share news and updates, and to express love and support. They can also be used to apologize, to forgive, or to simply say hello.

16.2 Format of INFORMAL/PERSONAL LETTER

- Address and Date
- Greetings and Name
- Introduction (Start with feelings/emotions and state the purpose of writing the letter)
- Body of the letter (Wh and How)
- Conclusion
- End Salutation with regards

Content of informal letter should answer:

WHAT, WHEN, WHERE, WHY, HOW, etc…

Opening for personal letters

1. You will never believe how happy I am to receive your letter.
2. How delighted I was when I received your letter!
3. I hope this letter finds you in great spirits!
4. My heart plunged into deepest ocean of sorrow (for some sad news)
5. What a splendid news you have shared! I want to offer my heartiest congratulations.

Closing for personal letters

1. I hope to hear the opportunity of meeting all of you. Kindly convey my wishes to your parents. See you soon.
2. For invitation: can't wait to see you! Isn't it sounding fine? We will have a great time, won't we?
3. I hope you will not be upset too long and will try to meet you as soon as possible.
4. Hoping that you are in the best of health and with the renewed sense of vigour, you achieve great pinnacles of success.

5. Your success has given me inspiration to increase my efforts and labours, so that I might get through and come with flying colours.

6. Believe me my dear friend these are merely not words but an expression of genuine sorrow. May god give you strength to bear the blow.

16.3 Examples:

Write a letter to your Friend asking him to be a part of spending Summer Vacation with you

Address

Date

My Dear ....,

I hope this letter finds you in the best of your health. You have not written to me for a long time. I think you must have been very busy with your examinations!

I am writing this letter to invite you to stay with me during the summer vacation. You must not have planned anything else yet, I suppose. Then why not spend a few happy days here with us all! My parents will also be very happy to see you in their midst.

I have chalked out a nice programme for us. Firstly, we will visit Aqua Park and the all-new Penguin Zoo. We will have fun at a place of your choice, if any during your short stay with us. It would be thrilling and interesting. The weather is fine these days. We can utilize our time by going to a nearby swimming pool and cycling too.

You will be happy to know my brother Ravi, has been employed as an artist at an FM Radio station. He takes part in children's programme and Radio-plays. One day we shall accompany him to the Radio station and go around the different studios. We shall also watch the rehearsals of the Radio-play. What a pleasure it would be for both of us!

I hope you won't disappoint me. Your company will be a boon to all of us. May I hope, you will start packing up immediately as soon as you receive this letter! Please do let me know.

Convey my sincere regards to your parents and love to Baby.

Awaiting your arrival,

Yours loving friend,

ABC

16.4 Banks:

1. You have been selected as the captain of your school's basketball team. Write a letter to your cousin in Pune telling him/her about it.
2. You went for a school trip to a hill station for three days. Write a letter to your grandmother telling her about it.
3. While visiting your uncle in Delhi, you witness the Republic Day Parade and see those children who are being given the Bravery Awards riding elephants in the Parade. Write a letter to your mother describing your feelings and how the sight will motivate you to do great deeds.
4. Write a letter to your brother who is at IIT Kanpur, describing the role you played in the Annual School play.
5. Imagine your brother is in boarding school. Write a letter to him about the new drama that you were a part of. Tell him about the preparation, audience feedback and role in detail.
6. Write a letter to a friend inviting him to accompany you on a trip to Jim Corbett National Park.
7. Write a letter accepting an invitation to accompany a friend to Jim Corbett National Park.
8. Write a letter to an aunt telling her about you winning an essay competition.

9. Write a letter to your friend thanking him/her for the gift you received on your birthday.

10. Write a letter to your father telling him about your new hostel and how much you like it.

11. Write a letter to your aunt telling her what you want for your birthday.

12. Write a letter to a pen-friend who lives abroad giving him/her personal details of your interests, hobbies, family and school life.

13. You have received an encyclopedia set as a birthday present from your cousin. Write a letter thanking him and telling him how much you appreciate the present.

14. Your friend has invited you to a party. Write a letter to him declining the acceptance of the invitation, giving your reason for not attending.

15. Write a letter to your friend who is still convalescing after a long illness.

16. Write a letter to your younger brother advising him to take part in games.

17. Write a letter to your younger sister recommending to her a few books which she should read.

18. Write letter to your father telling him about the profession you want to join after completing your studies.

19. write a letter to your mother describing to her your Annual Prize Distribution Function.

20. Write a letter to your younger brother who has fallen in bad company, advising him to give more attention to his studies.

21. You could not attend your friend's party because you had guests at home on that day. write a letter of apology, saying how much you missed the occasion. Ask your friend to send you copies of the photographs taken during the party.

22. You have moved to new city recently. You had promised to write to your friends about the new place within a month or so.

But for some reason, you were able to write to them only after three months. Write a letter of apology giving proper reasons.

23. Write a letter to your friend, telling him/her about an interesting place which you recently visited. Include details of names and descriptions to make your letter realistic.

24. Your NRI cousin is returning to India after 10 years. Write a letter telling her/him of the changes that have taken place in the country in the time that she/he has been away.

25. Your best friend and you had a quarrel over a misunderstanding. Write a letter to him/her, explaining the nature of misunderstanding and telling her/him that you two should get back together.

CHAPTER 17

FORMAL LETTER WRITING

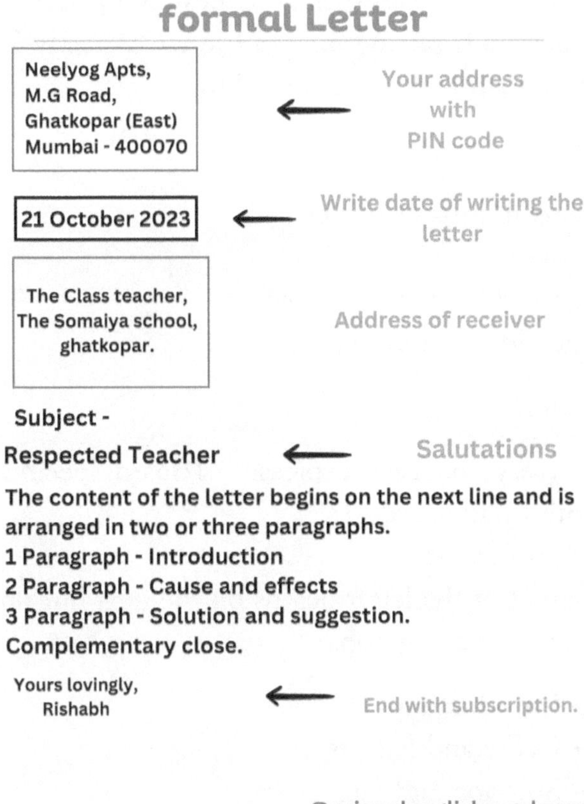

17.1 Introduction:

A formal letter is a type of letter written for a professional or official purpose. It is typically written in a formal style and follows a specific format. Formal letters can be used to apply for jobs, to request information, to complain about a product or service, or to simply communicate with people in positions of authority.

Purpose of writing a Formal Letter-

⇒ Formal letters are official letters written to people in their official capacity or written to a firm.

⇒ They are formal in nature. Nothing in such letters should be personal.

⇒ They deal with subjects such as request, complaint, loss or apology.

⇒ What matters is setting out your letter correctly, keeping to the point and maintaining the formal tone.

Format of Formal Letter

- Name and address of sender
- Date
- Name and address of addressee
- Mode of address or salutation

Dear Sir/Madam

- Subject (very concisely expressed) (Board specific/mostly done away with by all boards)
- Content of the letter
- The content of the letter begins on the next line and is arranged in two or three paragraphs

1 Paragraph – Introduction
2 Paragraph – Cause and Effects
3 Paragraph – Solution and Suggestion.

- Complimentary close
- Subscription –Yours faithfully/ Yours truly
- Signature of sender
- Name in capital

Opening for Formal

To Principal and Teachers,

1. I, undersigned and a student of grade ____ of this school, respectfully want to put forward the suggestion....
2. I would be extremely grateful to you if you could assist me in understanding...
3. I, on behalf of my classmates, desire to seek your permission (favour)....
4. With due respect, herewith I desire to request you to...

Closing

1. This is my humble suggestion and I hope you consider it since it will go a long way in fulfilling the objectives of education, which institutions like ours hope to achieve.
2. Kindly consider my request and let me know if and when it would be convenient for you to do the same...
3. I humbly pray for your consent and request you to...
4. I request you to give the matter due weight and deliberation.
5. We look forward to your consent for which we shall remain grateful.

To other officials and editor

Opening

1. Through the medium of this letter. I wish to express my concern over the....
2. It is a matter of grave concern to see that despite the...
3. I would like to draw your kind attention towards...
4. As a concerned citizen, I wish to highlight the issue of...

Closing

1. I request you to initiate the required move and take the desired step immediately.

2. I request your officials to wake from their slumber and apathy and help people in the hour of their greatest need.

3. It is therefore requested that a stringent action should be taken immediately to curb or eliminate this problem promptly.

4. I hope you will publish my letter in the columns of your esteemed newspaper so that the concerned authorities can look into this matter urgently.

17.2 Examples:

1]
A-26 Paschim Vihar,
Mumbai – 80.

14th September,2017.
The Editor,
The Times of India,
Mumbai -1.

Sub: Rising number of road accidents.

Dear sir,

Through the medium of this letter, I wish to express my concern over the increasing number of road accidents day by day. Road safety in our country is in a pitiable state.

A number of unnatural deaths take place almost every day and several become physically handicapped or permanently disabled due to road accidents. Most of the road accidents happen due to reckless driving. People in their hurry don't care to follow the traffic signals. The pedestrians tend to cross the roads from anywhere they want and are in turn hit by the speeding vehicles. The truck drivers, generally drunk, the young rash scooterists – all add to the number of road accidents.

A few strict steps like imposing fines and forfeiting the license of the offenders could stop the people from going wild on the road. Authorities need to be more stringent in issuing driving license. A constant checking and vigil are required.

I hope the concerned authorities and the general public will see the gravity of the matter and adopt some measures.

Yours truly,

Ridhima.

2] Write a letter to municipal commissioner complaining about the bad conditions of the road.

D-16, Sarojini Nagar,
Mumbai-80.
20th January,2017.
The Municipal commissioner,
The Municipal corporation.
Mumbai-80.

Sub – Bad conditions of roads.

Dear sir,

I would like to draw your kind attention towards pathetic state of roads in our area. For the last four months the road has been almost impassable. We have made several complaints but no action has been taken.

The road was dug up three months before for some pipe line work. It was not patched properly. The surface of the road has uneven layer of concrete which makes it extremely hard to drive on it. Heavy rains added to further woes creating pot holes which worsened the condition. This has resulted in slow moving traffic and even pedestrians find it difficult to walk on this road. During the rains, the road gets easily flooded.

I request you to take immediate steps to repair the road as it is one of the busiest roads of the area.

Thanking you,

Yours faithfully,

XYZ

4] Write an application to the principal of our school requesting him to arrange for an educational tour.

Your Address (not more than 4 lines)

15th April 20….
The Principal,
Govt. Boys High School,
Mumbai.

Sub- Arranging an educational tour.

Dear Sir,

I, on behalf of my classmates, desire to seek your permission to arrange an educational tour for students of grade VI.

Our school has a long and glorious tradition of benefiting its students through the arrangement of debates, seminars, group discussions, educational tours and other fruitful activities. These facilities rather fall among the salient features of our school. As no educational tour has yet been arranged it is the most appropriate time to do it now. All the students are eagerly waiting for the announcement of the same. It will give students a much-needed break from the classroom learning. It is a known fact that educational tours are of great educational value for students. They give us first-hand knowledge about some important historical places, cultural values, and educationally beneficial articles.

We would, therefore, like to go on an educational tour before the school breaks up for summer vacation. I humbly pray for your consent and request you to Please make it convenient for us to go on the tour.

Thanking you,

Yours faithfully,

XYZ

17.3 Lesson Plan /Induction activities/ teaching ideas:

- ➤ Begin by discussing the purpose of letter writing and why it's still relevant in today's digital age.
- ➤ Explain that there are two main types of letters: formal and informal, and each has its own set of rules and conventions.
- ➤ Show examples of formal letters on the whiteboard or handouts. Discuss the tone, language, and formatting used in these examples.
- ➤ Show examples of informal letters and discuss the tone, language, and formatting used.
- ➤ Assign topics to be practised by children in class.
- ➤ One similar topic can be given as home assignment.

17.4 Banks:

Practice questions for Formal letter

1. Write a letter to your teacher excusing yourself as you could not complete your project. Specify the reasons clearly.
2. Write a letter to the manager of your local post office telling him or her that you are shifting, and informing about your new address in which your mail should be sent to.
3. As Editor of the class 5 journal, write a letter to the principal of your school, requesting him to write a message for the students to be printed in the October issue of the journal.
4. Your class is organizing a tree plantation event on Earth Day. write a letter to the principal of your school, requesting him/her

to invite the Minister for Environment to be the chief guest on that day.

5. Write a letter to the editor of a newspaper on how we can protect our environment.

6. Write a letter to the principal of your school requesting leave to attend a wedding in your family.

7. Write a letter to the principal of your school requesting her to excuse you from upcoming examinations because you are unwell.

8. Write a letter to your class teacher requesting her to allow you to submit your science project later as you have been unwell for a week.

9. Write a letter to the principal requesting him to excuse you from paying the library fine.

10. Write a letter requesting your principal for permission to participate in an inter-school drawing competition.

11. Write a letter to your class teacher informing him that you have lost two of your course books. As the exam is approaching, request him/her if you can borrow any extra copies of the books which the teacher may have.

12. You have lost the library book issues to you last week. Write a letter to the librarian apologizing for the loss, and asking him/her how to make up for it.

13. You are recovering from an attack of jaundice. The doctor has advised you not to undertake any rigorous physical activity. Write a letter to the principal of your school requesting him to excuse you from games and PT classes for two weeks.

14. You are a member of the charitable organization, WE CARE, which provides free educational material to the children living in slums. Write a letter to the principal of Silver Bells Public School, appealing to students to donate their old textbooks and other school items to these children.

15. You read an advertisement in the newspaper about an organization called HELP THE AGED, which helps elderly and dependent

people. Write a letter to the president of the organization, asking him/her how you can help. You may ask for the program you can join, the services you and your schoolmates can provide, and the ways in which you can collect and donate money.

16. You came across an advertisement of a group that works for the conversation of the environment. Write a letter to the group leader asking him/her how you can become a member.

17. Classes 6 to 8 of your school have organized a fun fair to raise money for a community project. You need sponsors to donate prizes and snacks for your stalls. Write to a local business owner and ask for help for your project.

18. You saw an advertisement of a theatre group in the newspaper. Write a letter to the representative of the group telling her/him about your interest in theatre and asking how you can join them.

19. An essay-writing competition is soon to be held at the national level. Write a letter to the person organizing the competition to enquire how you may participate in it. Also ask about the criteria to enter the competition.

20. Write a letter to the editor of your local newspaper expressing your feelings about the proposal to convert one of the neighbourhood parks into a parking lot. You may write as an individual or on behalf of the children who live in your colony.

21. Write a letter to the editor of a newspaper expressing your views on environmental pollution.

22. As a trader, you had placed an order for 100 umbrellas of different kinds with a manufacturer. Write a letter to cancel the order. Give reasons for this cancellation.

23. Your father has been transferred to California to Los Angeles. Write a letter to the principal of your school, requesting him for the testimonial you will need for admission in a new school.

24. There has been a major theft in your colony. Write a letter to the SHO of your area police post regarding this theft.

25. Write a letter to principal of your school suggesting some improvements in your school library.

26. Mr. Rehman who bought a Vintech refrigerator recently, has lodged a complaint. The compressor of the refrigerator does not seem to be working. Mr. Rehman is angry not only because the refrigerator is not working, but also because the service department of Vintech has taken no action, in spite of his repeated calls.

    You are the services head of Vintech. Write a letter of apology to Mr. Rehman, promising him a replacement within a week. You will also offer one year of free maintenance worth Rs. 2000 for the refrigerator.

27. In the capacity of the Sales Manager of Electronics India, write a letter of apology to the customer, Mr. Rehman, for the faulty air-conditioner supplied to him.

    Assure him that he will soon get a fresh piece with a one-year warranty and free maintenance service.

28. Write a letter to the municipal corporation for cleaning roads.

29. Write a letter to electricity department requesting for restoration of electricity service.

30. Write an application to bank manager regarding a lost passbook.

17.5 Links for reference:

Links to the resources

Formal Letter Writing: Parts of a Letter, Important Points, Format and Samples of Formal Letter Writing - Smart English Notes

https://owl.purdue.edu/owl/subject_specific_writing/professional_technical_writing/tone_in_business_writing.html

https://ieltscanadatest.com/2017/11/5-things-you-need-to-know-about-tone-in-ielts-general-training-letters/

CHAPTER 18

ARTICLE WRITING

18.1 Introduction:

An article is a piece of writing which explicates ideas, thoughts, facts, suggestions and/or recommendations based on a particular topic. There are different kinds of articles, namely:

Expository article – The most common type of article which allows you to put out information on any particular topic without the influence of your opinions.

Argumentative article – An article in which an author poses a problem or an issue, renders a solution to the proposed problem and provides arguments to justify why their suggestions/solutions are good.

Narrative article – An article in which you have to narrate mostly in the form of a story.

Descriptive article – An article written with the aim of providing a vivid description that would allow the reader to visualise whatever is being described; using the right adjectives/adjective phrases is what will help you write a descriptive article.

Persuasive article – An article aimed at persuading or convincing the readers to accept an idea or a point of view.

Writing an article takes a lot of effort on the side of the writer. Content writers/creators, bloggers, freelance writers and copywriters are people who have mastered the art of article writing, without which they would not be able to make their mark as a writer of any kind.

Tips and Techniques

- In order to be able to write an article that makes sense in the first place, you have to keep a few things in mind.
- The first and foremost thing that you have to take care of when you are sitting down to write your article is to check if you are well aware of the topic you are going to write on.
- The second thing that you have to ask yourself is why you are writing the article.
- The next thing that you have to focus on is the kind of audience you are writing the article for because unless you know your audience, you will not be able to write it in a way that they would want to read it.
- The language you use is very important because, without the right spelling, correct grammar, punctuation and sensible sentence structure, the article would not be able to sell itself.
- Use keywords so that you get a good number of reading audiences.
- Maintain coherence within and between paragraphs.
- Double-check the data and information you provide, whatever the type of article it would be.
- Keep the title and description as short and catchy as possible.
- Edit and proofread before it is published.

18.2 Article Writing Format

An article must be organized in a proper way to grab the attention of the reader. It's important for the author or writer to first know the format of the composition and also mention the details consequently.

Title of the Article

Byline (Writer's Name)

Body (Main Part of the article)

Paragraph 1 (Introductive paragraph)

Paragraph 2 (Descriptive paragraph)

Paragraph 3 – Any additional information (if required)

Paragraph 4 – Conclusion (Ending part of the article)

Let us check the article writing format you should keep in mind while writing your piece of information.

Heading/Title

It is the first thing that eyes go on, to be noticed. It is the most important component of the format. The heading or title must be in accordance with the article. The heading of an article should be catchy and not more than 5-6 words. You can go as creative as you want to make it unique. The heading or title should be unique in such a way that the reader arouses their interest to read the whole article.

Byline

It refers to the name of the person writing the article. It is generally mentioned in the question. Do not mention your personal details.

Body

It is the main part of the article writing. It generally consists of 3-4 paragraphs.

Paragraph 1: It is always prescribed that you begin with a short introduction of the topic and its meaning to precise. Write in short, what the article is about by giving some quotations, that will be startling for the reader that will arouse some interest to read more.

Paragraph 2 or Paragraphs 2 & 3: Now, this is the part that can be written in either one or two paragraphs. You are required to do a complete analysis of the topic or subject matter given in the question. This paragraph may include:

The Problems – In how many forms does the problem exist?

The Current Scenarios – then you need to explain the current situation, the problems (if required), and whether there are preventive actions and betterment measures in the situation have been observed or not.

Advantages/Disadvantages – It may include advantages and disadvantages, depending on the topic in question.

Causes and Effects – Develop the cause-and-effect relationship by supporting it with facts or data. You can also write the consequences.

The Solutions- Write the solutions for the problem.

Paragraph 3 or Paragraph 4: The Conclusion/Ending. It is the concluding paragraph. It is important to conclude that you have started writing an article. Never leave your article open-ended, as it will create confusion for the readers. It is to be remembered that whatever you have elaborated on the problems, you always have to mention the steps taken the improve the situation and suggest some relevant suggestions as well. The paragraph needs to be short and precise. Here, also you can add some interesting quotes as well.

18.3 Sample Articles

Write a short article on Fashion shows or Children's dance competitions to show the features of an article to your students.

<u>REALITY BITES (Title)</u>

(Introduction)

Every television channel worth its value in salt does have a series of reality shows. If you don't host a reality show, then you aren't in the game. Singing shows, adventure shows, dance shows, comedy shows-you name it, they have it! Having children's singing and dancing competitions has become a trend. From Boogie woogie, Dance India dance to Dance plus and many more are really quite popular among the viewers. Reality TV shows involving children have become popular entertainment programmes in India. Many of these programmes are competitive talent hunts among children in various stages of childhood and adolescence. The shows "judge" children on talents such as dancing, stand-up comedy, and many others. Having said that, it is really a disturbing trend.

(Content)

Competitions are good as it helps one assess his or her potential, push oneself to excel and know where they stand among their peers. As long as it is healthy and it doesn't hamper with child's all-round development, it can be encouraged.

However, when these young kids in an impressionable age are subjected to face a media trial and undue pressure, it is heart breaking. TV talent hunts have proliferated in recent years, attracting high TRPs and making overnight stars out of tiny tots. Most of the time, the shows are not performance-based, but dependent on votes and popularity. The children feel pressurised because the whole world is watching them fail on television. Children are in a stage of emotional development where they are not emotionally equipped to handle rejection in a mature manner; and when they are not appreciated or fail to qualify, their mental state could affect the way they handle pressure situations for the rest of their life.

With glamour-struck parents living their dreams through their offspring, there is no respite for these young kids. They are deprived of a normal childhood. They miss out on normal education, play time and pursuing other hobbies.

Many of these reality shows for children create an unhealthy competition among children which affects them by enhancing their need for approval from the society.

In 2011, the National Commission for the Protection of Child Rights had issued guidelines for children participating in TV shows and advertisements, regulating working hours, prohibiting inappropriate roles and providing for adequate supervision. But nobody follows these measures 99% of the times. The Ministry of Information and Broadcasting (I&B) had issued an advisory for private television channels to ensure that children are not portrayed in an inappropriate way on performance-based reality TV shows.

(Conclusion)

It is the equal responsibility of the parents who driven by fame, money and glamour push their children into such whirlpool. They should avoid getting lured by this. As well the government should try to strengthen the existing self-regulatory mechanism and should issue a strong advisory to channels. We as a society need to address this issue and choose wisely whether or not to view such programs which lead to the exploitation of children. They are the future and they need to be protected.

A Day to Remember Our Dearest Teachers

The influence a teacher makes on an individual extends beyond the classroom. Teachers put in tremendous effort to understand their students and cater to them wholeheartedly. They take much care in moulding the character of their students, thereby helping them grow into compassionate and socially responsible individuals. Teachers' day is an occasion for us to remember our dear teachers and be grateful to them for the role they play in our lives.

A teacher is the building block on which a society is built. The responsibility of a teacher is huge as they perform the job of shaping intellectual and creative minds who turn out to be the future of society. In Dr. Radhakrishnan's opinion, "Teachers should be the best minds in the country". Celebrated in his honour, Teachers' day turns out to be a day to remember, appreciate, applaud and thank our teachers for providing us intellectual and moral guidance and support.

No matter how old we grow, there are a few teachers with whom we would like to share the progress we make in our lives, some who understand and believe in us more than our parents do, some whom we would run to no matter when and where we catch sight of them and some who turn out to be great friends apart from being wonderful teachers. Teachers' day is a chance to let these teachers know how much of an influence they have made in our lives. Sometimes, it is just another occasion; it is not necessary that you have to wait until Teachers' day to show your gratitude towards them for their constant love and support.

Contrary to all this is the present day, an age in which teachers are disrespected and disregarded for the kind of hard work they put into educating and empowering students, a day like this is absolutely necessary. It is a pain to see teachers being accused for various reasons, sometimes for no fault of theirs. In such an environment, Teachers' day can be a day for teachers to rethink their role and responsibilities as a teacher and for students to understand the importance of having teachers who really care for them.

<u>Article on Why We Should Stop Pollution and the Initiatives Taken to Curb Pollution</u>

There might be some people wondering about the need to stop pollution when the environment is not so much in ruins as people portray it to be. Well, the fact is that the environment is much more affected than any of us know. Controlling pollution will reduce health hazards, liability risk, economic losses; and provide us with clean air, better lifestyle, clear visibility, safe environment for all inhabitants of the Earth and so on.

Multiple efforts have been taken by the governments of various countries and organizations around the world to reduce the effects of pollution on our environment. One of the initiatives taken by the United Nations is the United Nations Environment Programme with the mission to inspire people all around the world to work together to care for the environment and take steps to improve the quality of life, not just for ourselves, but for the future generations as well. The United Nations has also designated June 5 of every year to be World Environment Day in order to bring representatives of all member nations together to address the environmental problems, to create awareness and to instigate action.

The answer to all the environmental problems the world is facing today is immediate action and consistency in reduced usage of private transportation, machinery with possible carbon emission and proper disposal of waste to start with.

<u>Digital Transformation – A Blessing or A Curse?</u>

Digital transformation has reached the ends of almost every human activity. From waking up in the morning, eating, working, relaxing to staying fit and healthy, everything has been digitised and made available. In a way, digital transformation has made life easier by helping us keep track of our body movements, eating and drinking habits. It has also made communication quick and simple. There are applications with the motive to never let us go hungry. All one needs is a good internet connection, the downloaded application, location and money to get food delivered at your doorsteps no matter which part of the country you are in.

Digital transformation has helped small scale and large scale businesses thrive by continuously keeping them on demand. It has also increased the efficiency of employees by creating ways to promote productivity and reliability. It has also made remote working conditions possible and comfortable.

However, there are some risks involved in this process. Though the whole idea of digital transformation is to help everyone equip themselves with access to the digital world, there are a lot of security and privacy issues that might come up as a result of data breaches and identity theft. It creates a shortage of skilled labourers in the fields of work that are based on digital technology. There are many other problems related to complete data loss and unsupervised expenditures, as online payments have made transactions a lot easier. Entertainment applications have increased screen hours and are likely to cause health problems.

To debate on digital transformation being a blessing or a curse would be an endless process. The aim of digital transformation and Digital India is only for the greater good of all human beings. The only aspect that every individual and ruling authorities have to take care of is that there is social and economic independence and security.

18.4 Lesson Plan:

Teaching students how to write articles is an essential skill that helps them express their thoughts, share information, and engage with various subjects. Here's a lesson plan to introduce article writing:

Objective:

By the end of this lesson, students will be able to understand the structure and purpose of articles, write a well-structured article, and apply writing techniques to make their articles engaging.

Materials:

> Whiteboard and markers
> Handouts with examples of articles
> Sample topics for writing practice

Introduction:

> Begin by discussing the purpose of articles and why they are important in conveying information, opinion, and engaging an audience.
> Explain that articles come in various forms, such as news articles, feature articles, opinion pieces, and more.

Structural Elements of an Article

Write the main structural elements of an article on the board:

> Headline: The title of the article that should grab the reader's attention.
> Lead: The opening paragraph that provides the most important information and hooks the reader.
> Body: The main content of the article, organized into paragraphs with each addressing a specific aspect of the topic.
> Conclusion: The closing paragraph that summarizes the key points or offers a concluding thought.

Discuss the purpose of each element and its role in the overall structure of the article.

Writing Techniques:

Explain various writing techniques used in articles, such as:

> Use of descriptive language: Using vivid and descriptive words to paint a picture in the reader's mind.
> Quotes: Including direct quotes from people relevant to the topic.

- ➢ Anecdotes: Sharing personal or other people's stories to make the article relatable.
- ➢ Facts and statistics: Backing up statements with credible data.
- ➢ Transitions: Using transitional words to smoothly move from one idea to the next.
- ➢ Provide examples and discuss how these techniques enhance the quality of an article.

Guided Practice:

- ➢ Hand out writing prompts or topics for articles. Ask students to choose one and start writing. Encourage them to follow the structural elements discussed and apply writing techniques.
- ➢ Circulate the room to provide assistance and answer questions.
- ➢ Sharing and Discussion: Ask a few students to share their articles with the class. Discuss the strengths and areas for improvement in their writing.
- ➢ Encourage constructive peer feedback.
- ➢ Editing and Revision: Discuss the importance of editing and revision. Explain the need to review their work for clarity, coherence, and grammatical errors.
- ➢ Provide some basic editing tips and techniques.
- ➢ Conclusion: Summarize the key points of the lesson and emphasize the importance of practice in improving their article writing skills.

18.5 Banks:

1. The number of women in the police force seems insufficient especially when we see the increasing involvement of women in terrorist activities. Write an article in 150-200 words for The Hindustan Chronicle', on the need of having more women in the police force.

2. In many parts of our country girls are still discouraged from going to school. Consequently, a sizable section of the population

is deprived of education. Schemes like Sarva Shiksha Abhiyan, CBSE scholarship to the single girl child and the Government's policy of giving free education to girls have come as a boon to our society. Write an article in 150-200 words on the education of the girl child in the country.

3. Advertisements have become a big business. They are promoted by celebrities drawn from various fields like films, sports, etc., leaving their influence on all people specially the young. Write an article in 150-200 words on 'The Impact of Advertisements on the younger generation'.

4. The present-day youth are greatly stressed due to cut-throat competition and consumerist culture. Write an article in 150-200 words on the causes of the stress on the modem generation suggesting suitable solutions.

5. As compared to the older generation the youth of today are greatly inclined to pursue adventurous activities either for money or for fun. There is a latest craze for joining reality shows, rafting, rock climbing, mountaineering etc. Write an article in 150-200 words on which life you would prefer—safe or adventurous.

6. India is standing at the threshold of joining the developed nations but that is not possible till we achieve complete literacy in the country. The contribution of students may be very significant in achieving our goals. Write an article in 150-200 words on 'The Role of the Students in Removing Illiteracy'.

7. Compulsory value-based education is the only remedy for inculcating values among the future citizens of the country. This will also help in the prevention of crime in the country. Write an article in 150-200 words on the need of compulsory value-based education.

8. Increase in the number of vehicles causes pollution and traffic jams. Write an article in 150-200 words for 'The New Indian Express', Delhi, highlighting the urgent need to solve these man-made problems, giving suitable suggestions. You are Madhav/Madhuri.

9. Corruption has become the order of the day. It has entered all walks of life. Write an article for your school magazine in 150-200 words on 'The Role of Youth in combating corruption'. You are Vijay/Vineeta.

10. India is said to be a young country and is emerging as a global power. The youth is getting increasingly concerned about the problems of corruption, environment, pollution, misuse of natural resources, etc. Write an article in 150-200 words on your vision of India in 2040.

11. Due to the globalization of food industry and fast food culture, traditional healthy diets are increasingly being replaced by unhealthy junk food containing artificial additives and preservative chemicals. Write an article in 150-200 words for a national daily on the need for inculcating healthy dietary habits.

12. Travel is an important part of a man's education. It enables a person to learn manners, customs, languages and history of different people and places and also widens the circle of one's acquaintances. Write an article in 150-200 words on "Travel, an Important Source of Education".

13. India is making strides in the field of technology. Technology has made life easier and more comfortable than it used to be earlier. At the same time people are turning to be more and more lazy and disease-prone. Write an article in 150-200 words on the disadvantages of too much of technology.

14. You are Keshav/Karuna, a social worker and counsellor. You are concerned about the stressed behaviour of both parents and students during the time of examination. Write an article in 150-200 words to be published in a local daily on 'Supportive parents and stress-free students' giving ideas to enhance healthy and meaningful PARENT- WARD rapport and for making the atmosphere relaxed and encouraging during examination time.

15. You are Keshav/Karuna, a social worker and counsellor. You are concerned about senior class students ignoring sports activities

owing to the pressure of examination and coaching classes. Write an article in 150-200 words to be published in a local daily on how sports not only promote physical fitness but also influence our scholastic achievements.

18.6 Sample Literature References:

Article on social media

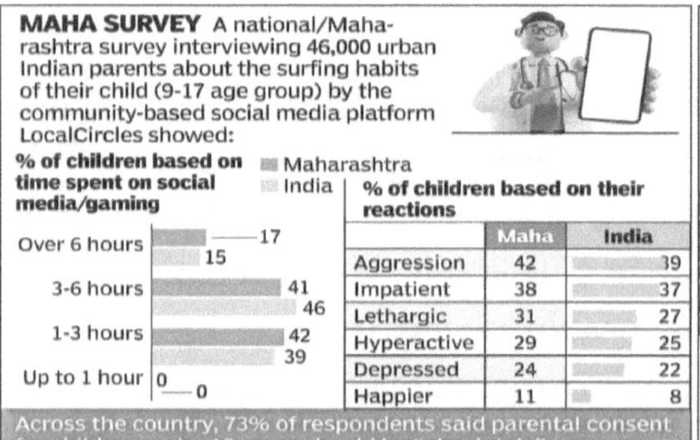

% of children based on their reactions	Maha	India
Aggression	42	39
Impatient	38	37
Lethargic	31	27
Hyperactive	29	25
Depressed	24	22
Happier	11	8

There is a growing epidemic of gadget addiction among youngsters, with a new national survey stating that children of up to 60% of those surveyed spent three to six hours a day on social media, OTT/video and online gaming platforms. The Centre is in the process of finalising a Digital Private Data Protection Law that mandates parental consent being sought for apps that are used by children under the age of 18

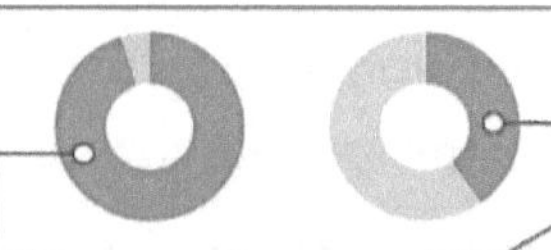

Mumbai: Six out of 10 youngsters in the 9-17 age group spend over three hours daily on various social media or gaming sites, according to a national survey interviewing close to half a lakh parents. In Maharashtra, 17% of the respondent parents said their children were online for over six hours every day. Incidentally, over three hours of daily social media interactions increases the risk of mental health problems such as depression and anxiety among children, according to US surgeon general Dr Vivek Murthy's 2022 report.

The survey, carried out by the community-based social media platform Local Circles, also found that children exhibited signs of aggression, impatience or hyperactivity after prolonged social media interactions. Almost a quarter of the parents in Maharashtra who participated in the survey said their child showed signs of depressive behaviour that is possibly linked to time spent on online interactions, while the corresponding number across India was 22%.

Only a tenth reported that their child was "happier" after play or social media time. The highest following was for OTT platforms, with almost 37% of the parents listing it as their child's favourite pastime; social media apps and online gaming followed closely. "Gadget addiction by children between ages 9 -18 has become the new reality," said Sachin Taparia of Local Circles. Online classes were the only option during Covid, but internet use by children for leisurely activities has only increased due to their urge to watch videos, play online games or connect with friends. The survey found that children also complained of headaches, back pain and anxiety due to the long hours spent in front of the screen.

He said the central government is in the process of finalising the new Digital Private Data Protection Law which mandates that parental consent should be sought for apps used by children under the age of 18.

Psychiatrist Dr Harish Shetty said social media is designed to be addictive. "But there is no denying that social media addiction, depression, loneliness and self-harm are related," he said.

According to the American Psychiatric Association's Diagnostic and Statistical Manual of Mental Disorders (DSM-5), gaming addiction has been identified as a mental disorder. However, parents are helpless when it comes to their child's social media use. "More than 40% of children in the general population are addicted to social media or gaming. We are clearly in the middle of an epidemic of gadget addiction. When there is an epidemic, we need public campaigns to bring about behavioural changes," said Dr Shetty. He gave the example of Mohityanche Vadgaon, Sangli, where every family switches off all gadgets at home for a certain period when a siren goes off.

CHAPTER 19

BLOG WRITING

19.1 Introduction

Blogging is a popular form of online communication where individuals or organizations share their thoughts, ideas, and experiences on a specific topic.

Blogs are typically written in an informal and conversational style, making them accessible and engaging to readers.

Effective blog writing requires careful consideration of various elements to create content that is interesting, engaging, and relevant to the target audience.

19.2 Elements of Good Blog Writing

A. Catchy Headlines

The headline is the first thing readers see and should be attention-grabbing and relevant to the content of the blog post.

Use action verbs, numbers, or intriguing questions to create compelling headlines that entice readers to click and read further.

B. Clear Organization

Structure the blog post with a clear introduction, body, and conclusion.

Use headings and subheadings to break up content and make it scannable and easy to navigate.

Ensure logical flow and coherence in writing, with each paragraph or section building on the previous one.

C. Engaging Content

Create content that is informative, interesting, and relevant to the target audience.

Use anecdotes, examples, and storytelling techniques to make the blog post engaging and relatable.

Incorporate descriptive language, vivid imagery, and sensory details to bring writing to life and connect with readers.

D. Appropriate Tone

Consider the target audience and purpose of the blog post when choosing the tone.

Strike a balance between being professional and approachable, depending on the nature of the blog and the audience.

Avoid offensive or derogatory language and be mindful of the tone conveyed in writing.

E. Unique Voice and Style

Emphasize the importance of authenticity and originality in blog writing.

Express your thoughts, ideas, and opinions in your own voice and style.

Discuss the value of personal storytelling and self-expression in blog writing while adhering to appropriate language and guidelines.

F. Use of Multimedia Elements

Enhance blog posts with multimedia elements such as images, videos, and infographics.

Choose appropriate and high-quality visuals that support content and engage readers.

Give proper credit for multimedia elements used and adhere to copyright laws and fair use principles.

G. Editing and Proofreading

Highlight the importance of editing and proofreading in blog writing.

Revise for clarity, grammar, spelling, punctuation, and style.

Read aloud or have peers review the blog post to catch errors or inconsistencies.

Value feedback and the iterative process of writing and revising.

19.3 Conclusion

Effective blog writing requires attention to catchy headlines, clear organization, engaging content, appropriate tone, unique voice and style, use of multimedia elements, and editing and proofreading.

Here are some blog sites that are popular among students and offer platforms for them to showcase their writing skills and share their ideas and opinions:

WordPress.com (https://wordpress.com/)

WordPress is one of the most popular blogging platforms, offering a user-friendly interface and customizable templates.

It allows students to create their own blogs, customize their design, and publish their writing easily.

Blogger (https://www.blogger.com/)

Blogger is a free blogging platform owned by Google, providing a simple and intuitive interface for creating blogs.

It offers a range of templates and customization options for students to personalize their blogs.

Tumblr (https://www.tumblr.com/)

Tumblr is a microblogging platform that allows students to create short-form blog posts, including text, photos, quotes, audio, and video.

It has a strong community of users and offers a unique blend of blogging and social media features.

Medium (https://medium.com/)

Medium is a popular online publishing platform that allows students to write and share their stories, articles, and essays.

It offers a clean and minimalist interface, and posts can be easily discovered by a wider audience.

Edublogs (https://edublogs.org/)

Edublogs is a blogging platform specifically designed for educational purposes.

It offers a safe and controlled environment for students and teachers to create and manage blogs, with features such as class blogs and student portfolios.

Kidblog (https://kidblog.org/home)

Kidblog is a blogging platform designed for students and teachers, offering a secure and private space for students to create and publish blogs.

It offers features such as moderation, privacy controls, and customization options suitable for young students.

Good bloggers to read

Certainly! Here are some popular bloggers who are known for their engaging writing and cover a wide range of topics:

Seth Godin (https://seths.blog/)

Seth Godin is a renowned author, marketer, and entrepreneur who writes about marketing, leadership, creativity, and personal development.

His blog features short, thought-provoking posts that offer insights and ideas for business and personal growth.

Joanna Wiebe (https://copyhackers.com/blog/)

Joanna Wiebe is a well-known copywriter and conversion optimization expert who writes about persuasive writing, copywriting techniques, and marketing strategy.

Her blog offers practical tips and strategies for improving writing skills and creating effective copy that drives results.

Maria Popova (https://www.brainpickings.org/)

Maria Popova is a writer and literary critic known for her blog Brain Pickings, which covers a wide range of topics including literature, art, philosophy, and culture.

Her blog features thoughtful essays that explore the depths of human creativity and curiosity.

Tim Urban (https://waitbutwhy.com/)

Tim Urban is a writer and illustrator who creates long-form, in-depth blog posts on a variety of topics ranging from technology and science to culture and philosophy.

His blog combines humor, storytelling, and research to offer unique and engaging insights on complex subjects.

Mark Manson (https://markmanson.net/blog)

Mark Manson is a bestselling author and self-improvement blogger who writes about personal development, relationships, and life advice.

His blog features candid and thought-provoking posts that challenge conventional wisdom and provide practical insights for living a meaningful life.

Zen Habits (https://zenhabits.net/)

Zen Habits is a popular blog by Leo Babauta that focuses on simplicity, mindfulness, and productivity.

The blog offers practical tips and strategies for simplifying life, building healthy habits, and finding balance in a busy world.

These are just a few examples of popular bloggers known for their engaging writing and thought-provoking content. Exploring different blogs can provide students with exposure to diverse writing styles, perspectives, and topics, helping them develop their own unique writing voice and style. It's always important to critically evaluate the content and consider multiple perspectives when reading blogs or any other online sources.

Here are some popular bloggers who create content specifically for kids:

Jeff Kinney (https://wimpykid.com/)

Jeff Kinney is the author of the "Diary of a Wimpy Kid" book series, which has been widely popular among kids.

His blog features updates on his books, behind-the-scenes looks at the illustrations, and interactive games and activities for kids.

National Geographic Kids (https://kids.nationalgeographic.com/)

National Geographic Kids is a website that offers educational content, games, quizzes, and articles about animals, science, geography, and more.

Their blog features kid-friendly articles, stories, and interviews with scientists, explorers, and experts.

Kids Activities Blog (https://kidsactivitiesblog.com/)

Kids Activities Blog offers a wide range of educational and entertaining content for kids, including crafts, recipes, games, and educational resources.

Their blog features articles, tutorials, and activities that are engaging and suitable for kids of various ages.

Science Buddies (https://www.sciencebuddies.org/)

Science Buddies is a website that offers science project ideas, resources, and educational content for kids interested in STEM (science, technology, engineering, and math).

Their blog features articles, experiments, and project ideas that are fun and educational, covering various science topics.

Kid World Citizen (https://kidworldcitizen.org/)

Kid World Citizen is a blog that focuses on global education and cultural awareness for kids.

Their blog features articles, stories, and activities that introduce kids to different cultures, languages, and global issues in a kid-friendly and engaging way.

Storyline Online (https://www.storylineonline.net/)

Storyline Online is a website that features popular children's books read aloud by famous actors.

Their blog features book recommendations, reading resources, and literacy-related articles that encourage kids to develop a love for reading.

These are just a few examples of popular bloggers who create content specifically for kids. It's always important for parents or educators to review and evaluate the content to ensure it is age-appropriate, safe, and aligns with their educational goals and values.

Indian bloggers:

Here are some Indian bloggers who create content specifically for kids:

Amar Chitra Katha (https://www.amarchitrakatha.com/)

Amar Chitra Katha is a popular Indian publisher of comic books and graphic novels that retell Indian mythology, history, and folktales.

Their blog features articles, quizzes, and interactive games that introduce kids to Indian culture, history, and mythology in a fun and engaging way.

Mocomi (https://www.mocomi.com/)

Mocomi is a website that offers a wide range of educational content, games, and activities for kids on topics such as science, history, geography, and more.

Their blog features articles, videos, and interactive activities that are tailored for kids and cover a variety of educational topics.

The Better India Kids (https://www.thebetterindia.com/kids/)

The Better India Kids is a blog that features positive stories, articles, and activities for kids that highlight the diversity, culture, and people of India.

Their blog features inspiring stories, interviews, and educational content that promote values such as empathy, sustainability, and social responsibility.

Kidsstoppress (https://www.kidsstoppress.com/)

Kidsstoppress is a popular parenting website in India that offers a wide range of content related to parenting, education, health, and activities for kids.

Their blog features articles, tips, and recommendations for parents and kids, covering various topics including books, events, and activities for kids in India.

Indian Moms Connect (https://www.indianmomsconnect.com/)

Indian Moms Connect is a blog that offers resources, articles, and activities for parents and kids, with a focus on Indian culture, traditions, and values.

Their blog features articles, stories, and activities that promote learning, creativity, and connection with Indian culture for kids.

Story Weaver (https://storyweaver.org.in/)

Story Weaver is an online platform that offers free, open-source children's stories in multiple languages, including many Indian languages.

Their blog features articles, interviews, and book recommendations that promote reading, storytelling, and language learning for kids.

CHAPTER 20

SPEECH WRITING

20.1 Introduction:

Speech Writing Format – In order to write a perfect speech, we must be well acquainted with the topic and must possess a wide range of vocabulary, a thorough knowledge of the subject, some research, and excellent organizational skills.

Here are the ideal format and tips to help you write your perfect speech.

A perfect speech must consist of:-

1. HEADING – The heading should be catchy and in not more than 5-6 words. You can go as creative as you want with this one.

2. OPENING LINE – This includes salutations, introduction, and the topic. Make sure you do not mention your personal details (name, school name, etc.).

Speech writing Example – Respected Principal, teachers, and my dear friends! Today, I (the name is given in the question) stand before you all to speak on the topic "(given in the question)".

OR you could start with a quote related to the topic and then go with the salutations and introduction.

3. BODY – It is the main part of your writing piece.

   i.   Then you need to explain the current situation, the problems (if any), and whether after any corrective actions, betterment in the situation has been observed or not.

   ii.   It may include advantages/ disadvantages depending upon the topic in question.

   iii.   Now here, it is important you follow a sequence. It is possible that you have too many points or very few points. When you have a lot of varied points, it is better you choose a few best ones and write a line on each. In case you have very few already, explain them in at least two lines each.

   iv.   You have to strictly follow the prescribed word limit in a limited time frame so just do not go on writing and writing.

   v.   MOST IMPORTANT- Always begin with your strongest point. You can accommodate the weaker ones in between and end with another strong point.

   vi.   Feel free to give your personal opinion in one or two lines.

   vii.   It is very important that you do not deviate from the topic. There are chances you may get ideas linking from one to another that may deviate you from the main point. You have to refrain from doing so.

4. SOLUTION/CONCLUDING PARAGRAPH – Now, it is to be remembered that wherever you elaborate a problem, you always have to mention the steps being taken to improvise the situation and suggest a few solutions as well.

Now, it would be great if you could add a few quotes relating to motivating the people to take action.

Here also, the rule of STRONG-WEAK-STRONG applies.

5. Last but not the least, the concluding line, thanking the audience for their cooperation and their patience. It is very important to conclude what you've started. Never leave a speech or for that matter, any of your answers open-ended.

Tips on Speech writing –

1. Make sure you use language which is suitable for the audience you are addressing. Usage of complex vocabulary for addressing children is not advisable.

2. Usage of quotes is highly recommended. Quotes can be used at the time of commencement or as an ending statement. A quote in the middle of the speech would also be fine.

3. Make sure you write in paragraphs.

4. Practice previous year question papers.

5. Read as many samples as you can. It will give you an idea as to how they are actually written.

6. Read newspaper editorials or opinions. They give new ideas and opinions that may help during exams.

7. Plan before you pen. Just make a list of all your important points on the rough sheet (last sheet of your answer booklet) so that you do not forget relevant points while writing. This also helps you in maintaining a sequence, which is very important.

8. The presentation is very important.

9. Make sure you double-check for grammatical accuracy and spellings. They carry marks.

10. Always have a few general quotes in handy. They help in the presentation and show that you're prepared.

Sample writing

1. As Mukul / Mahima of Alps Public School, write a speech to be delivered in school assembly highlighting the importance of cleanliness suggesting that the state of cleanliness reflects the character of its citizens.

SPEECH WRITING: IMPORTANCE OF CLEANLINESS

Suggested value points:

- Importance of Cleanliness – School, home & Surroundings
- Present status
- Prevents diseases
- Need to practice?
- Reflects the character of the nation
- Benefits of Cleanliness
- Conclusion

IMPORTANCE OF CLEANLINESS.

In the words of the great John Wesley, "Cleanliness is next to godliness".

Good Morning respected principal, teachers, and my dear friends. Today, I, Mukul/Mahima, stand before you all, to highlight the importance of cleanliness.

Cleanliness is the state or quality of being clean or being kept clean. It is essential for everyone to learn about cleanliness, hygiene, sanitation and the various diseases that are caused due to poor hygienic conditions. It is crucial for physical well-being and maintaining a healthy environment at home and at school. An unclean environment is an invitation for a lot of mosquitoes to breed in and spread deadly diseases. On the other hand, not maintaining personal hygiene leads to a lot of skin problems and decreased immunity.

The habits learnt at a young age get embedded into one's personality. Even if we inculcate certain habits like washing hands before and after meals, regular brushing and bathing from a young age, we are not bothered about keeping public places clean. For this, on 2nd October, 2014, the Indian Prime Minister launched a nation-wide cleanliness campaign, "*Swachh* Bharat" to provide sanitation facilities to every family, including toilets, solid and liquid waste disposal systems, village cleanliness, and safe and adequate drinking water supply. Teachers and students of schools are joining this 'Clean India Campaign' very actively with great fervour and joy.

Good health will ensure a healthy mind, which will lead to increased overall productivity resulting in higher standards of living, thus developing the economy. It will boost India's international image. Thus, a clean environment is a green environment with less people falling ill. Cleanliness, hence, is defined to be the emblem of purity of mind.

Thank you.

2. The recent rise in incidents of violent behaviour of students is a matter of concern for all. The problem can be curbed if students learn how to manage anger. Write a speech on the topic in 150-200 words to be delivered in the school morning assembly.

Answer

HOW TO MANAGE ANGER

Honourable Principal, Respected teachers and my dear friends, today I would like to share with you few "Ways to Manage Anger".

The growing intolerance among the new generation resulting in violence towards teachers is a matter of grave concern. The old-age guru-shishya Parampara is losing its sheen. Aggressiveness in students may be triggered by several things: as a self-defence reaction, stressful situation, over-stimulation or lack of adult supervision.

It has become the need of the hour to curb the situation. Life skills classes shall be inculcated in the time-table. Teachers should be given training to handle such defiant and hostile behaviour. Meditation and deep breathing also help and thus, should be practiced every morning. Students must be taught to count till 10 before reacting in anger. Also, sessions on anger management and it's far-reaching importance must be held.

Remember, Anger is one letter short of danger. It makes it all the more important to be able to diffuse one's anger. It's never too late to begin because a wise man once said,

"For every minute you remain angry, you give up sixty seconds of your peace of mind."

Thank you.

3. Write a speech in 150-200 words on 'Benefits of early rising' to be delivered by you in the morning assembly of your school. You are Karuna/Karan, Head Girl/Head Boy.

BENEFITS OF EARLY RISING

Honourable Principal, Respected teachers and my dear friends, today I, Karuna/Karan, your Head Girl/Head Boy stand before you all to highlight the far-reaching "Benefits of Early-rising".

"Early to bed and early to rise, makes a person healthy, wealthy and wise."

The words of Benjamin Franklin have been backed by science. It has been proved that morning people are persistent and proactive. It leads to better performance, greater success, and higher standards of living. Rising up early also relieves stress and tension because it gives you the time to squeeze in a workout before you get distracted. This is why; morning people tend to be healthier and happier as well as have lower body mass indexes.

For this, one needs to maintain a proper schedule and has to go to bed on time. You should restrict the usage of gadgets immediately before going to bed and these tiny steps will help you become an early riser. Researchers have also said that early morning is the best time to study and gain knowledge. This will help you in staying ahead in the class and keep your grades up. Most entrepreneurs are early risers as they believe it is the key to a successful, happy and content life.

Hence, if you don't develop a habit of waking up before the rest of the world, you won't be able to change the world.

Thank you.

CHAPTER 21

PICTURE COMPOSITION

Picture composition is a form of creative writing that involves describing or narrating a picture in words. It helps students to develop their observation, imagination, and language skills. A picture composition can be written in different ways, such as a story, an account, or a description, depending on the picture and the purpose of the writing.

21.1 Introduction:

Introduce the topic and the objectives of the lesson. Explain what picture composition is and why it is important. Show some examples of pictures and ask the students to identify the main elements, such as characters, setting, action, etc.

- Observe most of the individuals/characters in the picture. Observe their clothes, expressions, accessories etc.
- Observe their activities – What are they doing?
- Most importantly note/mind the "mood" of the character looking happy, tired, bored, excited?
- Mind the age and gender of the characters!
- Look for surrounding things – like TV, books, background (if it's a scenery) etc.
- Background might be a closed room, might be a beach, a school, a farmland etc. Comment on the relevance of the place, the background and connect it to the characters in the picture.
- Try to derive a meaningful relation among the individual characters, and try to speak about most of the characters/ things etc.

- Give appropriate title to the picture.
- Add adjectives and adverbs.
- Use brilliant vocabulary.

Activity 1:

Divide the students into groups and give each group a picture. Ask them to brainstorm ideas for writing a picture composition based on the picture. They can use different techniques, such as listing, mind mapping, freewriting, etc. They can also create their own title and theme for the composition.

Activity 2:

Ask each group to choose one idea and write an outline or a draft of their picture composition. Remind them to follow the basic structure of an introduction, a body, and a conclusion. They should also use descriptive language, sensory details, and literary devices to make their writing more interesting and engaging

21.2 Sample Picture Examples:

Q. Look at the pictures and write a picture composition:

A day at the Beach

> Golden beach, serene sea, blue vast sky, mighty mountains, Shining sun, buoyant birds
> Children and their activities – building sand castle, flying kites, playing ball, splashing water, relaxing, free like birds, fluttering like butterflies etc.
> Their mood and expression – happily, cheerfully, enthusiastically, gleefully, twinkling eyes, grinning wide, happy faces, jumping with joy etc.
> Relevance – maybe it's a holiday, Sunday, school trip, summers etc.
> Conclusion – going to beach is fun
> Title – Sunny day, A Day at beach, Family's fun outing.

(Always note the points and then write the composition)

A scene at an airport

CHAPTER 22

REPORT WRITING

A report is essentially a formal document focused on a particular topic, encompassing information, discoveries, or outcomes derived from an investigation or research process

What is it: A piece of writing that reports. Also includes recounting, retelling, commenting on people incidents ideas, general truths on nature, situations of cultural social interests.

Types: newspapers, articles, minutes, brochures, event reports, textbook

Purpose: Report real events and current affairs. Accuracy is aimed for.

Tone: Formal and Often neutral but not always.

Language and grammar: passive voice. Regular chronological sequencing is used. Past tense in reporting.

Structure of the report:

a. Introduction (main facts, WH and How)

b. Body (key ideas and supporting details which can be facts, examples, statistics, explanations, reasons)

c. Conclusion (evaluation of facts, results, future action).

Arrange the Paragraphs in logical order.

Requirements:

Wh and How questions are answered

Brief and to the point with no digressions of elaborate descriptions

causes and effects are established

Sample Report

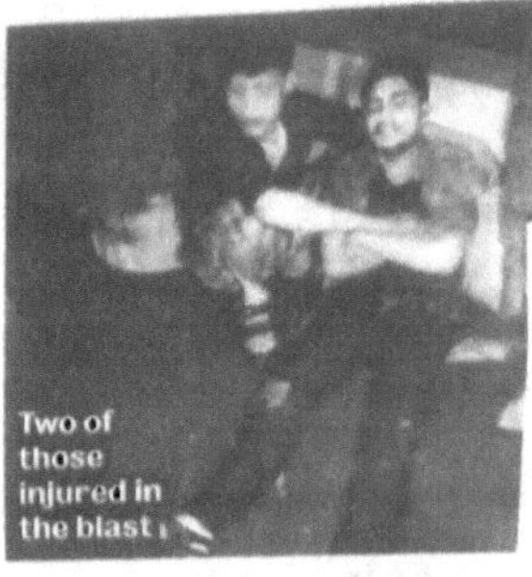

One killed, four injured in blast at Boisar factory

Massive pressure in the reactor of the chemical unit caused the explosion, say cops

| Somendra Sharma & Vinay Dalvi
mirrorfeedback@timesgroup.com

TWEETS @MumbaiMirror

One person was killed and four others were injured in an explosion in a reactor of a chemical factory in Boisar MIDC area of Palghar district late Monday evening. The police sources claimed that the explosion occurred due to massive pressure that had accumulated in the reactor of the unit.

Those injured have been identified as Mohammad Mohsin Altaf, 30, Dilip Gupta, 28, Umesh Kushwaha, 22, and Pramod Kumar Mishra, 35. The deceased has been identified as Sandeep Kushwaha, According to the Boisar police,

around 7:30 pm, a massive explosion took place in the chemical unit of Nandolia Organic Chemicals Pvt Ltd, situated at Boisar MIDC Plot T-141. The impact of the blast was felt in nearby villages such Salvad, Tarapur, Chichani, Boisar and Parasatal. Soon after the explosion, the police team, fire brigade officials, MIDC and Maharashtra Pollution Control Board (MPCB) officials reached the spot.

According to a police officer, the operator of the reactor, Sandeep Kumar Singh, told the police that making of a chemical product was under way, and while the distillation was on, the pressure in the reactor increased, leading to an explosion. Those who were working in the unit were injured and rushed to Thunga Hospital in Boisar.

The officer said there were 14 people in the unit, of which four

Two of those injured in the blast

were hospitalised.

"As of now we have registered an accidental death case. The MIDC and MPCB officials are carrying out their investigation, and once they give their opinion as to what actually caused the explosion, we would take further legal action," the officer said.

"Thankfully, the incident took place during change of shift at the chemical unit, and hence not many people were present there," Boisar Panchayat Samiti member Mukesh Patil told Mumbai Mirror.

Sample Report writing

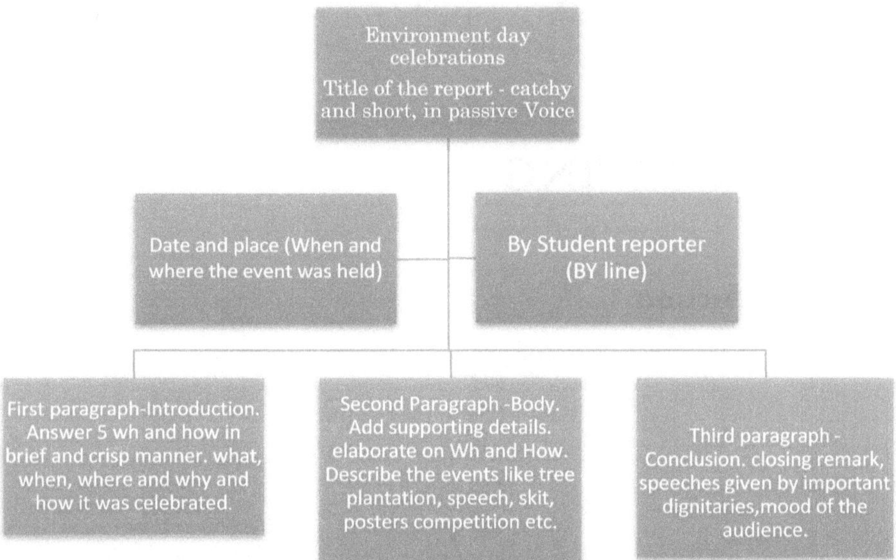

CHAPTER 23

STORY WRITING

23.1 Introduction:

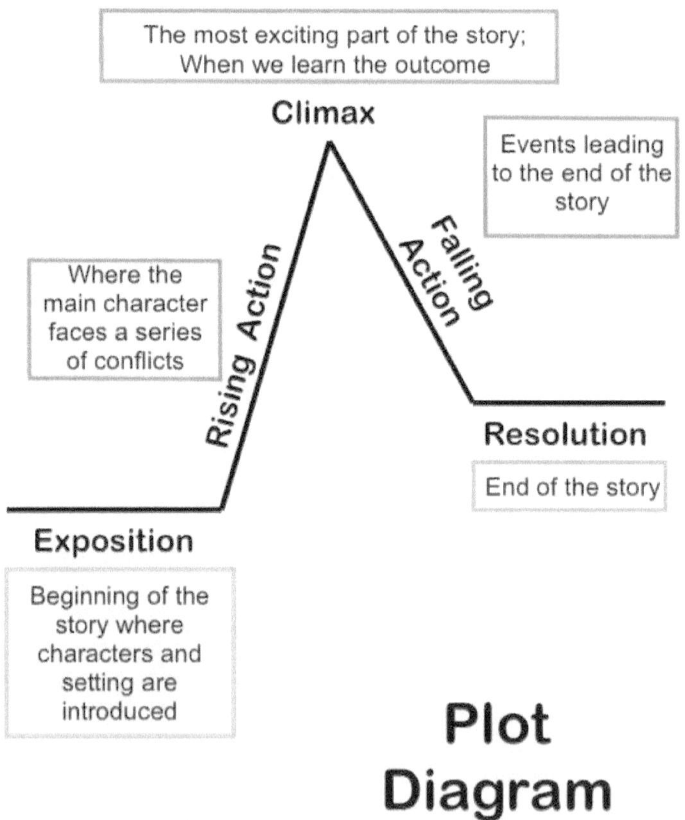

What is a story writing?

A story writing is narrating of 'real or imaginary events' involving real or imaginary people.

It is usually written in "easily understandable grammatical structure" with "natural flow of speech".

The key elements (or stages) of a Story Writing are as follows-

- Title
- Character
- Setting
- Plot
- Conflict
- Resolution
- Theme/message

Setting of the story should be made.

- ➢ Time, location, context and atmosphere should be described to create imagery.
- ➢ The setting is often decorated with descriptions of scenes such as super market, bedroom, crowded metro train, or drizzling evening…

Characterization - Identify 2 - 3 main characters and a few supporting characters in the story.

- ➢ Traits, physical features, age, profession, how the character is viewed by others.
- ➢ It could be a living person, a dead person, a ghost, an imaginary character, a robot, a dog, a toy… unlimited list.

PLOT

Plot is flesh and muscles of story writing. It comprises events and characters' actions. More creatively you describe and logically connect the events and actions, stronger the plot would be; and stronger the plot you create, better interest would it generate among readers.

It contains:

Problem and solution

Conflict (with self, others, nature, things)

Resolution (How the character resolves the problem/conflict, mystery or surprise revealed)

Conclusion

How the loose ends tie up in the end.

What happens after the conflict is resolved.

Few more things to remember:

- Add dialogues
- Generally, story is written in past tense.
- Use appropriate tense when writing dialogues.
- Use imagery to create vivid picture

➢ (What the reader can see, hear, smell, taste or feel)

Most importantly DO NOT FORGET TO GIVE APT TITLE TO YOUR STORY

Use figurative language like simile, metaphor, personification etc (don't overdo it)

Outline Story

1. Read the outline of the story carefully and understand what the story is all about.
2. Develop the points of the story into complete sentences.
3. Follow the sequence in which the points are given. These points form the series of the events.
4. Do not omit any part of the outline.
5. Do not include unrelated or unnecessary events that may change the story completely.
6. Every story has a beginning, middle, and an ending.
7. Include details to make story interesting and enjoyable to read.
8. Write the story in the past tense, even if outline provided in present tense.
9. Introduce dialogue or conversation to make the story interesting.
10. Use direct speech when introducing these conversations.

Direct speech: The ant looked up at the dove and said, "Thank you for saving my life. I am very grateful."

Indirect speech: The dove told the ant that she should climb up on the leaf and that it would keep her safe.

Title of the Story:

- ✓ Choose the title of the story that is related to the main characters or events of the story.
- ✓ Write the title using title casing, in which the main words begin with capital letters. E.g., The Ant and the Dove
- ✓ Avoid use of quotation marks and punctuation marks in the title unless it is a sentence

Always make a story map before actually writing the story.

23.2 Sample writings

1. The Mysterious Island

Once upon a time in a village of Rampur there lived three best friends Ram, Akhil and Tina their friendship was so close that nobody could separate them. They loved to solve mysterious and go tracking and have fun. One day as Tina was going to the market, she heard a faint growl before the soil/ground.

She got curious to know what was there beneath the soil. She rushed to tell Ram and Akhil." Well get ready for another mystery" Tina Tingled with joy" Mystery?

Ram and Akhil asked. Yes oh! Just pack your bags and get ready I will tell everything along the way" She answered

As they reached the place where Tina had heard the growl again and this time it was louder as if the thing was coming towards them. They began digging faster and as they were digging. Rams spade fell inside the hole they had dug and it hit something hard. Then all of the three jumped in the hole and began searching Rams spade but it was nowhere to be seen. All of a sudden, a fire got lit up on the entrance of a cave. The 3 got curious to go inside the cave. As they went in the cave a bright light shone towards them and in a jiffy, they entered and Island.

A soothing sound was being played behind. There was a large hotel and an-ice skating ring there was even a restaurant which had legs to walk and hand to cook. They enjoyed very much and as they returned; they found the spade lying there where if had fell." How did the spade come there? They wondered and who was making the faint growl?

– Ayushi Dedhia

2. Write a story that involves car chase, a barking dog and an old trunk.

The mystery of the missing child "Aah!" George Fayne Shrieked. Nancy Drew who was driving passed an expensive car and a little scratch appeared on the door. Luckily, they didn't notice and sped away. "I don't understand why you cannot relax while I drive. Do you have to shriek so that I scratch thousands of cars like these? Nancy yelled. She was with her chums (friends)-Bess interrupted with a twisted face and blinking eyes. Does that car read 9432. Nancy wondered aloud ignoring them. Is it the same red car which robbed the bank and took a missing child with them? Nancy pondered with her eyes. wide and one eyebrow up. Without hesitating she started following the car. George & Bess were astonished but did not say anything as Nancy passed through cars. zigzagging through bikes and breaking the signal. Nancy was on a wild goose chase. OR more like a wild car chase. The red car stopped suddenly and parked it. Nancy parked her convertible too and cautiously signals her friends to come out. Both of them understood that she was on a mystery. The men got out of their car looking really suspicious. Nancy and her chums hid behind the tree waiting for the men to do something. The first man whispered "You go get the rope. I guard ".The other man proceeded. Cold chills ran down George's spine. Bess shivered. Nancy suddenly, saw a dog and had a Nancy-brilliant idea. She went close to the dog, which was sleeping, and stepped on its tail gently. The dog roared and starting barking. The man who was on guard, moved slowly to the tree with a confused face and wrinkled forehead. Meanwhile her friends rushed to the red car and dragged a truck out which was at the back of the car. They yanked it to the blue convertible and stocked it to the blue convertible and stocked it inside the truck. Nancy making a move, sat on the seat and her friends got inside too. She started the car and they sped away." Whew!" Bess let out a sigh. "What an adventure!"

An adventure is oh no! yet to come." Nancy grinned. As expected,the man rushed in and started following Nancy's car. She beamed and drove to be police station. The red car was after her and driving like crazy. The car stopped short when it realised where it was. George and Bess got out swiftly and caught hold of the man who was trying to escape. They held the man and after a quick talk with Mr Andrews, the policeman who knew them so well, threw the man in jail. They handed over the trunk to them too.

"The other man escaped," Nancy grunted. "What a pity!" After they got them and ate something, Bess inquired, "Do you know what was in the trunk?" "Yeah," George continued. "A missing child!" What a pity!" Bess shrieked. "The poor child must be starving." "Bess, you only think about food all day along?" Nancy put a question forward. "No," Bess said mischievously. "Sometimes I think about desert too!"

– Nishka Shah

3. Brave Explorers

It was chilly winter morning in the month of December. Today was Christmas day. The houses of the town Hawed were so thickly decorated with lights and Christmas trees and mistletoe that they couldn't be seen behind their makeup. Children were throwing snowballs at each other as if they had guns and were making snowman's with bright orange carrots and Rooty coal.one of the snowy roofed houses belonged to the Sharma's.

The Sharma's had two children, John and Lucy. John was a brown-haired boy with blue eyes, smooth skin and even teeth. He had an adventurous attitude and always wanted to do something new. His sister Lucy had darker hair, but the blue eyes and adventurous attitude was the same. They lived in a small cottage with small, square windows and a big, wooden door whose fingers were rusted. Their BBF, Jack lived next door. That morning the twins wanted to go exploring the 'brave of secrets'. They had a map of that cave in their bedroom and it was for treasure. They asked their mother who said 'Sure go but don't yet lose'. They raced out of the house and called Jack who was snoring in his bed. It took a while for him to wake up. soon they were on their way John his nose buried in the map.

They entered the cave and john began to decipher the map. They walked through the twisting tunnels and doodled the stalagmites and stalactites. On their way they took a wrong turn into a dark tunnel. Bats fluttered over their heads and screeched in their ears. The eager John hadn't looked at the map properly and they became lost in the maze. Suddenly Lucy said "Look over there!" They had come to a big rock blocking their way. Jack took a stick he had got with him and began to poke it at few small rocks at the top. The rocks gave away so there was a hole on top. They quickly scrambled up the and out. When they all reached the other side, their jaws dropped to the floor they were in a chamber full of gold coins, sapphires and a ruby encrusted cup. before anyone could speak Jack said" This is the cup of the Queen of England! We need to tell the police. There is an opening over there let's go through.

After coming out they saw daylight! They raced to the police station and poured out their story and gave the inspector the map. Few policemen took them home and calmed down the panic – sprockets parents. They chatted a lot and the police saluted and left. The children went out and began to play with the snow pleased about finding the treasure. They played in bliss.

– Ura Swami

How The Forest was Saved.

The golden rays of the sun filtered through the tall pine trees and fell on the ground. The birds were chirping and the water in the distant stream was gurgling. Aarya and Aarav were panting and stopped to catch a breath. Their grandpa followed them, " Come on! You young cubs. Getting tired so easily. We still have to walk for anotherhalf an hour to reach our cottage." This was their every sunday routine- taking trails in the nearby woods.

Aarav and Aryaa were sibling who lived with their robust grandpa ever since their parents passed away in an accident. Being an ex- forest officer grandpa loved forests and he considered animals and trees as his friends. He had instilled the same love in the kids too. Aarya and Aarav too loved animals and had three pets- two dogs and one parrot. They both were quite adventurous and never missed an opportunity to go an adventure. They lived in a beautiful cottage nears the Sanna forest.

One night, after the day's work they were sitting by the fire. Grandpa was reading a book to them. Suddenly they heard shrieks and cries. And then there were gunshots. Grandpa immediately understood what was wrong. The kids were scared and worried for their forest friends. They all immediately grabbed their torches and grandpa grabbed his gun and they ran towards the noise. By the time they reached, there was nobody. "Who can that be?" asked Aarav. Grandpa whispered, " It has to be the hunters. They might have killed the deer and taken their skin. We have to do something to stop them."

The next day grandpa called the police and informed them what happened. The police asked grandpa to help them. As grandpa had lived there for a long period of time, he was well- versed with the whole forest. They had to lay the trap to nab those hunters. Aarya and Aarav quipped in chorus, "We will also help you, grandpa."

Hence, they decided and went ahead with the plan. Before the nightfall, they went to the same place in the forest. They lay a huge net and covered it with the dry leaves. They tied the end of the ropes to the nearby tree. Now they needed to put a bait for the hunters. They tied a goat to a stick. Then they all hid behind the bushes and waited patiently for them to come.

At nightfall, they heard the footsteps. They sat in hushed silence. As the hunters approached, the grandpa alerted the police officer. As he signalled, the officer was supposed to pull the ropes and trap the hunters. The hunters were trapped.

The news of how a grandfather and his two grandkids saved the beloved animals of Sanna forest spread far and wide. They were given many awards of appreciation. Grandpa said, " Animals have equal rights as we humans."The kids beamed proudly and promised to always take care of their forests.

Grade 6 (collective work)

23.3 Lesson Plan/ Induction activities/Teaching ideas:

Objective: By the end of the lesson, students will be able to create a well-structured narrative story with a clear beginning, middle, and end.

Materials Needed:

- ➢ Whiteboard or chart paper
- ➢ Markers
- ➢ Story starter prompts or images
- ➢ Paper and pencils for each student

Lesson Plan:

Introduction (15 mins):

- ➢ Engage: Everyone loves stories. It can be in any form- visual, verbal, written or just to listen. This is one creative writing topic which is thoroughly enjoys by the kids and adults alike.
- ➢ You can begin by taking up any story. You can watch the story, read aloud to the children or narrate a story or ask them about their favourite stories.
- ➢ Begin with a discussion about what makes a good story. Ask students about their favourite stories and what elements they think are essential for a captivating tale.
- ➢ Then bring out the elements of story writing gradually by discussing with the students. Explain what is setting, characters, plot, conclusion, theme etc,.

- ➤ Define: Explain the basic structure of a story (beginning, middle, and end) and the importance of characters, setting, and plot. Explain and teach them how to make a story Map using the organiser.

Activity 1 - Brainstorming Ideas (15 mins):

- ➤ Story Starters: Provide story starter prompts or images to ignite their creativity. Encourage them to pick one and brainstorm ideas individually or in groups.
- ➤ Share Ideas: Ask students to share their ideas with a partner or in small groups. This helps in refining and expanding their concepts.

Activity 2 - Planning the Story (20 mins):

- ➤ Storyboarding: Introduce the concept of storyboarding. Distribute papers and ask students to draw a simple storyboard with boxes for the beginning, middle, and end of their story.
- ➤ Character and Setting: Have students describe their main character(s) and the setting in their story using the storyboard.

Activity 3 - Writing the Story (30 mins):

- ➤ Writing Time: Encourage students to start writing their stories using their storyboards as guides. Remind them to focus on descriptive language, character development, and a clear plot progression.
- ➤ Peer Review: Pair students up for peer review. They can exchange stories and provide feedback to each other focusing on what they liked and any suggestions for improvement.

Activity 4 - Presentation and Reflection (10 mins):

- ➤ Sharing Stories: Allow some students to volunteer to share their stories with the class. This helps in boosting confidence and encourages creativity.

- ➢ Reflection: Lead a discussion about what they learned during the process and what they found challenging or enjoyable about writing their stories.
- ➢ Conclusion (5 mins): Summarize the key points discussed during the lesson and emphasize the importance of practice and revision in improving their storytelling skills.

<u>Homework (Optional)</u>: Encourage students to refine and edit their stories based on the feedback received and bring the final draft to the next class.

This lesson plan aims to engage students in the creative process of storytelling while also providing opportunities for collaboration and self-reflection. Adjust the timing and activities according to the class's pace and needs.

Explain students that stories they write can be of various genres.

There are numerous genres of stories, each with its unique characteristics and elements that appeal to different audiences. Here are some common genres:

- ❖ <u>Fantasy</u>: Involves magical or supernatural elements, often set in imaginary worlds with mythical creatures or magical powers. Examples include "Harry Potter" and "The Hobbit."
- ❖ <u>Science Fiction</u>: Focuses on futuristic technology, space exploration, time travel, or scientific advancements. "Star Wars" and "The Martian" are examples.
- ❖ <u>Mystery</u>: Involves solving a puzzle or crime, often with unexpected twists and suspenseful elements. Agatha Christie's "Murder on the Orient Express" is a classic mystery.
- ❖ <u>Adventure</u>: Takes characters on exciting journeys or quests, often involving danger, action, and exploration. "Treasure Island" and "The Adventures of Tom Sawyer" fall into this category.

- ❖ <u>Historical Fiction</u>: Set in a specific historical period and often weaves fictional characters and events into real historical contexts. "Percy Jackson & the Olympians" series is an example.
- ❖ <u>Realistic Fiction</u>: Stories that could happen in the real world, featuring everyday life, relationships, and experiences. "Wonder" and "Bridge to Terabithia" are examples.
- ❖ <u>Fairy Tale</u>: Often includes magical elements, usually with a moral or lesson and featuring archetypal characters like princes, princesses, witches, and talking animals. Examples include "Cinderella" and "Snow White."
- ❖ <u>Folklore</u>: Stories passed down through generations, often rooted in cultural traditions and legends. "Anansi the Spider", "Panchatantra", "Jataka tales" etc,. stories are examples.
- ❖ <u>Horror</u>: Intends to scare or unsettle readers, often involving supernatural elements, monsters, or psychological terror. "Dracula" and "The Shining" are examples.
- ❖ <u>Romance</u>: Focuses on a romantic relationship as a central plot, exploring themes of love, passion, and relationships. "Pride and Prejudice" and "The Notebook" are examples.
- ❖ <u>Mythology</u>: It encompasses a body of traditional stories, often of a sacred or religious nature, that explain the origins of a culture, its deities, heroes, rituals, and sometimes the natural world.

These genres can overlap, and stories often contain elements from multiple genres. Exploring various genres helps writers understand different storytelling styles, themes, and audience preferences, allowing them to broaden their creative horizons.

Help students with appropriate vocabulary and terms required to write various genres.

23.4 Question Banks:

Outline Story:

King Bruce- king of Scotland- lost a battle- ran away in a cave- spider in cave- trying to reach at the top- falling again and again – did not give up- finally reached at the top at the seventh attempt- king Bruce learnt a lesson - he went and fought bravely.

Sample Story Map

- ➤ Title – Never give up, The Spider's lesson, The King who learnt a lesson
- ➤ Characters- King Bruce and the spider
- ➤ Setting- Scotland, cave
- ➤ Problem and solution – king is losing the battle, the spider teaches him a lesson
- ➤ Moral- Try and Try till you succeed, never give up, winner never quit and quitters never win, fall down seven times get up the eighth time.

To be included-

- ➤ One simile
- ➤ One alliteration
- ➤ One show not tell
- ➤ Two dialogues
- ➤ Character description
- ➤ Brilliant Vocabulary

1. Fox sees crow with a piece of cheese in its beak – starts talking to the crow – flatters the crow – crow is impressed – opens beak to sing – cheese falls down – fox eats it – moral
2. Wolf wanted to eat the sheep – couldn't eat due to shepherd and guard dogs – wore sheep's skin – walked among the sheep – sheep

started to follow it – wolf led the sheep far from the herd – ate the sheep – moral

3. Grasshopper singing and chirping – sees an ant working hard – ant was collecting food for winter – grasshopper tells ant to sit with him – ant refuses – continues to collect food – in winter ant has plenty of food – it distributes food to everyone – grasshopper has no food – goes hungry – moral

4. Young girl gets lost on the wat to school – scared, but decided not to panic – meets helpful people on the way – one of them is a girl who is her sister's age – lends her a phone – young girl calls mother – explains where she is with the help of new friend – parents come to pick her up – praise for her smartness and quick thinking – thank friend who helped her

5. On his way to school, boy sees poor man – finds out he is an educated man, but homeless – decides to help him – takes him to his father – father gives him a job – man is grateful – stays with the family for many years

6. Going to school – see spaceship – shocked – want to run away – forced to enter the ship – aliens offer tea and snacks – ask for information about earth – vanish soon after – parents don't believe when brought to the spot where spaceship was – worried about too much pressure of studies – were aliens real? – planning an alien invasion?

7. Boy lived with grandfather – was disobedient – opened gate – duck and cat escaped – bad wolf attacked – robin flew around wolf's head – wolf was tired – grandfather chased wolf – peter was sorry

8. Got a silver coin from grandfather – promised to take care of it – description of coin – how it got lost – how you got it back – your feelings

9. Day of results – Rashi nervous and tense – mother encourages – Rashi returns from school – very upset – not fared well –

disheartened – loses interest in school – one day in the garden – an ant trying to drag bread crumb – tries again and again – does not give up – Rashi understands – moral

10. Saurav – good badminton player – works hard – believes he is strong mentally and physically – selected for inter-state coaching camp, leading to selection of best player of the year – excited – father cautiones him not to get over-confident – at camp meets Bhaskar, a player with hearing impairment – dismisses him – Bhaskar wins the championship – Saurav learns valuable lesson of life

11. A jester – the king's favourite – enjoys great freedom – once offends the king – condemned to death – pleads for mercy – is asked to choose how to die – wants to die a 'natural death'

Prompt Story:

1. Shanti was walking down the dark lane when suddenly…
2. Akhil was at the camp with his friends and there…
3. Ravi was climbing the neem tree when his foot slipped and…
4. I still remember the day when all my friends were home…
5. The moment I woke up in the morning, I knew it was a special day…
6. Pranay had been very quiet for the past few days.
7. My grandmother is possibly the funniest person I have ever known.
8. Sometimes, human beings can learn from animals.
9. Today, a new girl joined our class. Her name is Arshi.
10. For two years, Ramya had seen the old balloon seller standing at the same spot every day on her way back home from school.
11. The moment I woke up, I knew something was wrong…
12. Radha was walking on a lonely street when suddenly…
13. Nayan was reading his book when he heard his sister screaming…
14. My mother was working in her office when she saw the man…
15. Shalini heard the glass break as soon as she turned around…
16. Naina was alone at home talking to her friend on the phone when suddenly she thought she heard her father calling her…
17. In a world where memories could be bought and sold, I stumbled upon a market selling forgotten dreams…
18. The old, dusty book sat on the shelf for years, untouched, until one rainy afternoon…

Picture story:

1. Look at the following pictures and write a picture story for each of them:

2.

3.

4.

23.5 Short Story Rubric (Self-Assessment)

Title of story:

When you write a story, use these criteria to check whether you have covered most of the elements of the story.

A. Content and Organization

Criteria	YES	NO
1. **Characters:** Are the characters well-developed? Do they have *thoughts, feelings* and *actions*?		
2. **Setting:** Is the setting (time and place) described clearly? Is the setting appropriate?		
3. **Use of dialogue:** Do the characters speak? Are the conversations realistic?		
4. **Plot structure:** Are the events well sequenced? Is there a problem and a solution, climax and conclusion?		
5. Does the story end in a logical way? Does the main character learn a lesson? Is there a twist?		

Comments:

____

____

B. Use of Language

Criteria	YES	NO
1. **Vocabulary:** Is there a wide range of descriptive words and phrases? Have you used appropriate idioms or proverbs if required?		

Criteria	YES	NO
2. **Grammar:** Is the story told in the past tense? Do the verb tenses all seem to be correct?		
3. **Use of literary devices:** Are there examples of devices like simile, metaphor and alliteration?		

CHAPTER 24

HOW TO WRITE A DIARY ENTRY

Diary entry is one of the creative writing question asked to assess the student's creativity, expression and imagination. (and of course grammar …that goes without saying.)

It can cover range of topics which express joy, fear, hurt, shock, agitation or an experience.

The tone or the mood of the diary is earnest, sentimental, confessional or contemplative.

Diary can be written in narrative, descriptive, poetic style.

24.1 Format of the diary

Place

Day and date

Time

Greetings (optional)

First paragraph – Express your feeling and state the purpose of writing this diary entry. (Imagine as if you are having a conversation with your diary)

Second paragraph – Give details. (Five W's and one H works well for this paragraph). Explain what happened, when and where it happened, who was involved, with whom, how it happened,why it happened etc.

(Please note – you need not give all W and H all the time. It will depend on the topic)

Third paragraph – Close with your final thoughts on the topic. if possible add a future course of action in the given situation.

Closing remarks

Sample diary entry

Mulund

Monday, 11 June 2020.

10.00 p.m. (here or right hand side)

Dear Diary

The most amazing thing happened today ! You would hardly believe it. I got selected for the final round of the inter- school singing competition. It has always been my dream and now I am over the moon. (Feelings and purpose)

Since the day this competition had been announced, I was excited about it. You know very well, how much I love to listen and sing songs. I enrolled myself and practised day and night. Initially I was confused as to which song should I sing. Thankfully, mom was of great help. She helped me pick a beautiful song that suited my voice. First round of selection was among the students of our school. There were four other competitors. Each one was equally good. Today was the first round of selection, I was jittery. I had butterflies in my stomach just before my performance. When I heard each one sing, I thought I am not going to make it. Nonetheless, I tried to remain positive. When our music teacher came on the stage, my fingers were crossed. Finally, she announced my name. I couldn't believe my ears. I was jumping with joy. Everyone congratulated me. (details – What, when, how why etc)

I am going to practise harder now for the finals. I will give my best. Mom has promised to buy a new karaoke for me if I win. That would be like icing on the cake. wish me luck. I am off to bed now. See you tomorrow. (Future course)

Shriya (your name)

Remember, coherence of your thoughts is important. You start with PRESENT events, go to Past and end with FUTURE.

CHAPTER 25

EXPANSION OF IDEAS

It can include proverbs, adages or ideas or situations of social relevance.

To explain an entire situation in a sentence, to elucidate one's character in a few words or in short to make anything crisp, proverbs were invented The value of the proverbs lie in their applicability and usage even today from time immemorial, even though the world has undergone many cultural and traditional metamorphoses from time to time.

For effective expansion writing, you should clearly understand the essence of the proverb or the idea. Thus, the purpose of a proverb or idea expansion is to expand on the meaning of a particular proverb and find its application in life.

The expansion can be divided to three parts. The first being introduction, the second being expansion and the third being conclusion.

So, how do we go about it?

Whenever an idea or proverb is given, first understand the key words and their symbolic meaning or idea associated with it.

For instance; 'Cut your coat according to your cloth'. So, the key words here are coat and cloth.

Literally, it means you cannot stitch a coat of your liking if you do not have enough cloth. In broader sense, coat stands for your needs and wants and cloth stands for the resources you have to meet those needs and wants. So, you need to limit your needs as per the resources you have and you cannot indulge in extravagance beyond your means.

Hence, in the first paragraph – Explain the literal and symbolic meaning, add an anecdote if any you have. Anecdote can be real, imaginary or anything you might have read or seen somewhere. (Aesop's fables, Panchtantra and other moral stories come in handy for this).

Second paragraph – Elaborate the idea! Add examples from real life or situations. If you cannot think of any real situations or examples, create hypothetical situation. If you are a student, you can give examples related to student life. Mention stories of inspiring personalities.

If I have to expand "Where there is a will, there is a way'. I can add examples related to a hardworking student, write about personalities or great leaders like Mahatma Gandhi, Ratan Tata, Sachin Tendulkar, Steve Jobs etc.

Mention any facts and figures if you know or if it is needed.

Here, you can also add a counter view or an argument to the given proverb. There can be a contrasting opinion which also needs to be written about.

To illustrate- "Pen is mightier than the sword "is an opposing view to "Action speaks louder than words".

Third paragraph - Reiterate the meaning of the idea. State the related proverbs and add quotes by famous personalities to drive home the point. End it with appropriate conclusion.

"Stitch in time saves nine" is related to "Time and tide waits for none", "Procrastination is the thief of time",etc.

"It's really clear that the most precious resource we all have is time." – Steve Jobs. (Quote by famous personality)

Remember the order:-

1. First state the meaning of the proverb or idea; literal as well as symbolic. Add a short story or an anecdote related to it.
2. Next, add examples to elucidate further;real or imaginary simplify it further by giving examples of real life situations.
3. Then, add a counterview or contrasting opinion.

4. Finally, sum it up, conclude it with related quotes and proverbs.

Remember – 'Rome was not built in a day'. To master the art of Expansion of Idea, you will have to read, build a bank of quotes and stories and practise it to perfect it. And of course, don't forget to be coherent and grammatically sound!

Sample writing

LAUGHTER IS THE BEST MEDICINE

(First paragraph – Introduction with anecdote)

On my way to school daily, I pass through a garden. Every morning, it is filled with cacophony of various sound and noises. In one green corner of the garden, a group of senior citizens, all dressed in their best exercise wear, were laughing cheerfully, their hands falling up and down in rhythm. They were all part of a Laughter club- a unique club with a mantra of laugh your way to health. Laughter is the best and the cheapest remedy there is to keep us physically and mentally fit. *"There is nothing in the world so irresistibly contagious as laughter and good humor." — Charles Dickens, A Christmas Carol.*

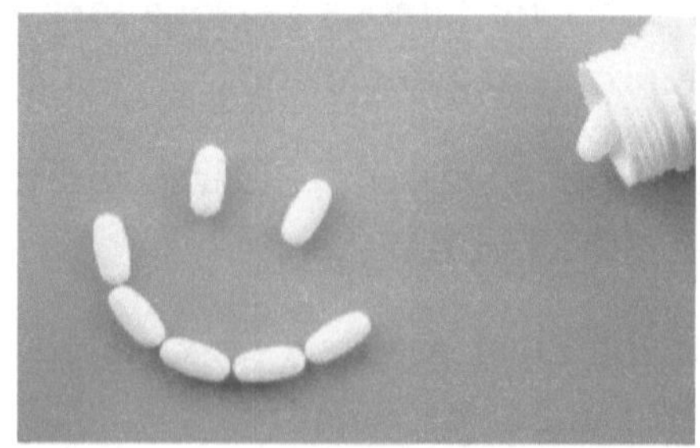

(Second paragraph – Elaborate with examples, facts and figures)

It is a scientifically established fact that laughter produces hormones in our body and arms us with disease resistant powers. A good laugh chases the toxins out of our system and makes us feel greatly refreshed and happy. No doubt, for that reason comedy shows, movies and serials are so popular.

Studies have shown that a kindergarten child laughs around three thousand times a day where as an adult merely laughs on an average around seventeen times a day.

Pulling a long face pushes us down deeper into misery and prolongs our suffering. laughing loudly, heartily, boisterously gets us out of gloom and makes us see sweetness and sunshine everywhere around us.

Laughter is the medicine for many ailments, feeling of depression, fear and anxiety.

(Third paragraph – Counterview)

This is not to say that laughter is literally a cure all and can replace particular drugs and medicaments. For a patient down with serious ailment, laughter does not mean uproarious merry noises; rather a certain attitude towards physical ailment; a certain lightness of heart and joviality of mind; a certain buoyant optimism. Such a psychological state is immensely helpful in driving away disease and distempers.

(Conclusion – summing up with related quotes and proverbs)

An optimist laughs to forget; a pessimist forgets to laugh. Health is actually true wealth and let us take care of this wealth with large doses of smiles and laughs every day. To quote Mark Twain- "Against the assault of laughter, nothing can stand".

CHAPTER 26

JOURNALING AND ENGLISH LANGUAGE LEARNING

Imagine a space where you can say what you want, write whatever your heart tells, vent out all your feelings and emotions. Won't it be nice? Where you aren't judged, admonished or unheard…

Well, your journal or diary is just that space for you. Diary writing or Journaling is as old as hills.

In simple terms, Journaling or Diary writing means to write without any inhibitions. It's a great way to explore your surroundings and make connections with yourself. It is exploratory and not directive. It is writing without any strict guidelines or rules.

This simple exercise can help you master your language skills and at the same time it can become a beautiful personalised learning journey for you.

Why journaling for language learning

1. Journaling can help improve not only your writing but your other language skills as well. Every time you write in English, you practice using new vocabulary you've picked up and remember grammar rules you've learned. It's a good vocabulary mining exercise as you describe people,places and events,you learn relevant vocabulary.

2. You also hone your thought patterns when communicating in English – how you arrange your ideas, the way you come up with the appropriate words/terms and arranging them in order – these become clear to you as you construct sentences and read what you write every day. The more you write, the better you'll be at expressing yourself in English.

3. Many artists practice what they term as "stream of consciousness" writing to unlock their creative potential. This is simply writing whatever is on your mind every morning right after waking up. This will help you unblock ideas and make your thoughts more free.

4. It enhances your fluency. The kind of thoughts that flow freely while journaling can carry over wonderfully to your conversations. It will make you more fluent while you are expressing your thoughts and ideas to others.

5. It can become a tool that brings more awareness to learning English. As a matter of fact you can create an exclusive English learning journal. The journal can have sections specially dedicated to vocabulary enrichment, creative writing and grammar learning and improvising.

How to go about it:

- **Time** – schedule your own quiet time to think and write. It can be a short as 5-10 minutes before you start work in the morning or before you sleep at night. Find a place where you feel comfortable and you won't be distracted.
- **Something to write on** – You can write on a notebook, a diary, your computer or mobile device. **Just start !!! (I would prefer pen and paper any day)**
- **Set a goal** – Some people start by writing 100-200 words per day, some less. It will be up to you but it's good to have a goal in mind to keep you on track.
- **There is no age limit to start.** Anyone can start at any age or time.

What should you write about?

➢ Anything and everything!
➢ You can write about your day, about what you experienced, learned or discovered.
➢ Write about your dreams, plans and goals.
➢ Write a letter to someone (or to an imaginary person).
➢ Describe someone or something you love, or hate.
➢ Some people start a gratitude journal to remember how blessed they are.
➢ Others keep a dream journal to understand their thoughts.
➢ You can go big by writing whole paragraphs or start small by writing bulleted lists.
➢ You can even add drawings or sketches if you feel like it. It shoud reflect your personality. KEEP IT REAL!

The important thing is that you write down your thoughts in a simple and coherent manner.

Things to remember when journaling:

➢ You don't have to be a poet or a novelist. Don't worry about grammar, spelling or style for the moment. It doesn't have to be great writing. You will improve as you go.
➢ Be honest and authentic.
➢ Starting can be hard. You will be tempted not to do it on some days. Do your best to stick with it. If you miss one day, make sure to take it up again in the following days.
➢ Read what you have written at the end of the week and take note of what you have learned about yourself. You can choose to do this weekly, monthly or not at all. However, it is important to note that you will gain more insight about yourself and your language skills if you re-read your entries at some point.

Through a journal, you can set goals and keep track of your progress. If you decide to write the journal by hand, even better, as that will make you more focused on the words you write.

Journaling is a great way to encourage yourself to write. You should do it daily for the best results.

What do Leonardo Da Vinci, Albert Einstein, Winston Churchill and Anne Frank have in common? They all kept journals! This is not a surprise as studies have shown that journaling is an effective tool to fire up creativity, improve critical thinking and aid in decision-making.

Remember, 'We write to taste life twice, in the moment and in retrospect.' – Anais Nin.

Sample text from The Diary of Anne Frank

SUNDAY. JUNE 14, 1942

I'll begin from the moment I got you. the moment I saw you lying on the table among my other birthday presents. (I went along when you were bought. but that doesn't count.)

On Friday, June 12, I was awake at six o'clock, which isn't surprising. since it was my birthday. But I'm not allowed to get up at that hour, so I had to control my curiosity until quarter to seven, When I couldn't wait any longer, I went to the dining room, where Moortje (the cat) welcomed me by rubbing against my legs. A little after seven I went to Daddy and Mama and then to the living room to open my presents, and you were the first thing I saw. maybe one of my nicest presents. Then a bouquet of roses, some peonies and a potted plant. From Daddy and Mama I got a blue blouse, a game, a bottle of grape juice, which to my mind tastes a bit like wine (after all, wine is made from grapes), A puzzle, a jar of cold cream, 2.50 guilders and a gift certificate for two books. 1 got another book as well. Camera Obscura (but Margot already has it, so I exchanged mine for something else), a platter of homemade cookies (which I made myself, of course. since I've become quite an expert at baking cookies), lots of candy and a strawberry tart from Mother. And a letter from Grammy, right on time but of course that was just a coincidence.

Then Hanneli came to pick me up, and we went to school. During recess I passed out cookies to my teachers and my class, and then it was time to get back to work. I didn't arrive home until five. since I went to gym with the rest of the class. (I'm not allowed to take pan because my shoulders and hips tend to get dislocated.) As it was my birthday. I got to decide which game my classmates would play. and I chose volleyball. Afterward they all danced around me in a circle and sang "Happy Birthday." When I got home. Sanne Ledermann was already there. Ilse Wagner, Hanneli Goslar and Jacqueline van Maarsen came home with me after gym. since we're in the same class. Hanneli and Sanne used to be my two best friends. People who saw us together used to say, "There goes Anne, Hanne and Sanne." I only met Jacqueline van Maarsen when I started at the Jewish Lyceum, and now she's my best friend. Ilse is Hanneli's best friend, and Sanne goes to another school and has friends there.

They gave me a beautiful hook, Dutch Sasas and Lesends. but they gave me Volume II by mistake, so I exchanged two other books for Volume I. Aunt Helene brought me a puzzle, Aunt Stephanie a darling brooch and Aunt Leny a terrific book: Daisy Goes to the Mountains.

This morning I lay in the bathtub thinking how wonderful it would be if I had a dog like Rin Tin Tin. I'd call him Rin Tin Tin too, and I'd take him to school with me, where he could stay in the janitor's room or by the bicycle racks when the weather was good.

CHAPTER 27

GRAPHIC ORGANIZERS

Graphic organizers are visual tools that help individuals organize and represent information in a structured and easily digestible format. They can be very helpful while we do various creative writing topics.

Graphic organizers provide a clear visual representation of concepts, relationships, and ideas. They help learners make connections between different pieces of information, making it easier to understand complex topics and retain information.

Here are various types of graphic organizers, each with its unique purpose and design:

- **Mind Maps**: These radial diagrams start with a central concept and branch out into subtopics, making them excellent for brainstorming and organizing ideas.
- **Concept Maps**: Concept maps are similar to mind maps but focus on showing relationships between concepts through linking lines and labels.
- **Flowcharts**: Flowcharts are used to represent processes and decision flows. They use shapes and arrows to depict the sequence of actions and decisions.
- **Venn Diagrams**: Venn diagrams are used to compare and contrast two or more sets or concepts, showing overlapping and unique characteristics.

> **Timeline Charts**: These organizers display a sequence of events over time, making them useful for history and project planning.

> **KWL Charts:** These are used to organize what a learner Knows, Wants to know, and has Learned about a particular topic, aiding in pre- and post-learning assessment.

> **Cause and Effect Diagrams** (Fishbone or Ishikawa Diagrams): These diagrams help identify the root causes of a problem or the effects of an event.

> **Spider Maps**: Spider maps start with a central theme and radiate into subtopics, providing an organized way to explore a central idea or question.

> **T-Chart:** T-charts are used for comparing and contrasting two different aspects of a topic.

Depending on the form of writing, one can use any of these organisers for organising and arranging ideas and give structure to their writing:

1. Sequence Chart

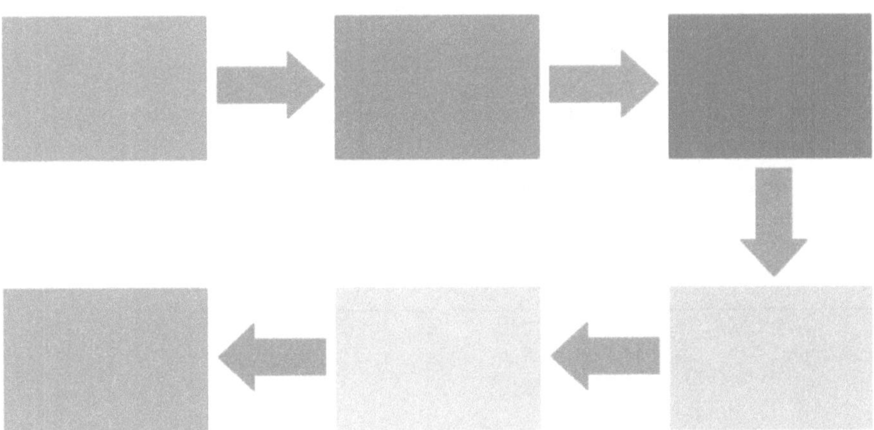

2. Story Map

Name ____   Date _______________________

Story Map 2

Write notes in each section.

Setting:
Where:

When:

↓

Major Characters:

Minor Characters:

↓

Plot/Problem:

↓

Event 1:

Event 2:

Event 3:

↓

Outcome:

3. Mind Map

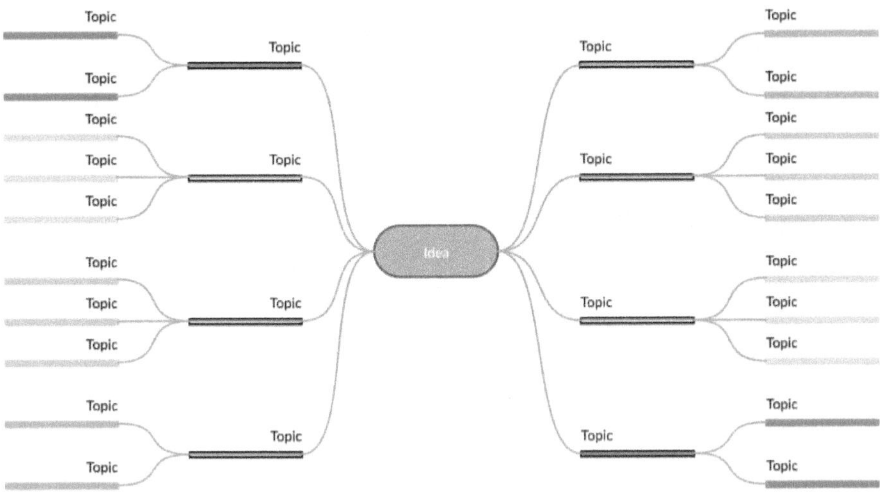

4. Venn diagram

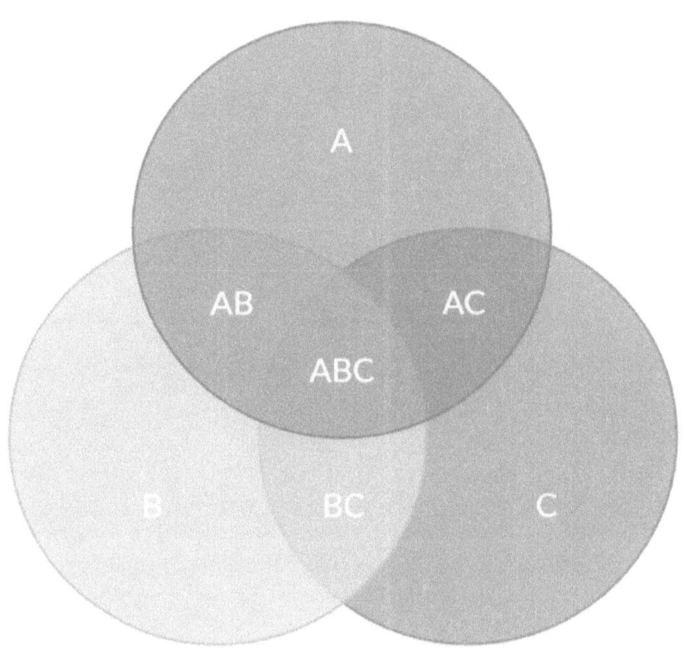

5. STORY MAP

Setting:
Where:
When:
Major characters:
Minor characters:
Plot / Problem:
Event 1:
Event 2:
Event 3:
Outcome/ Resoulution:

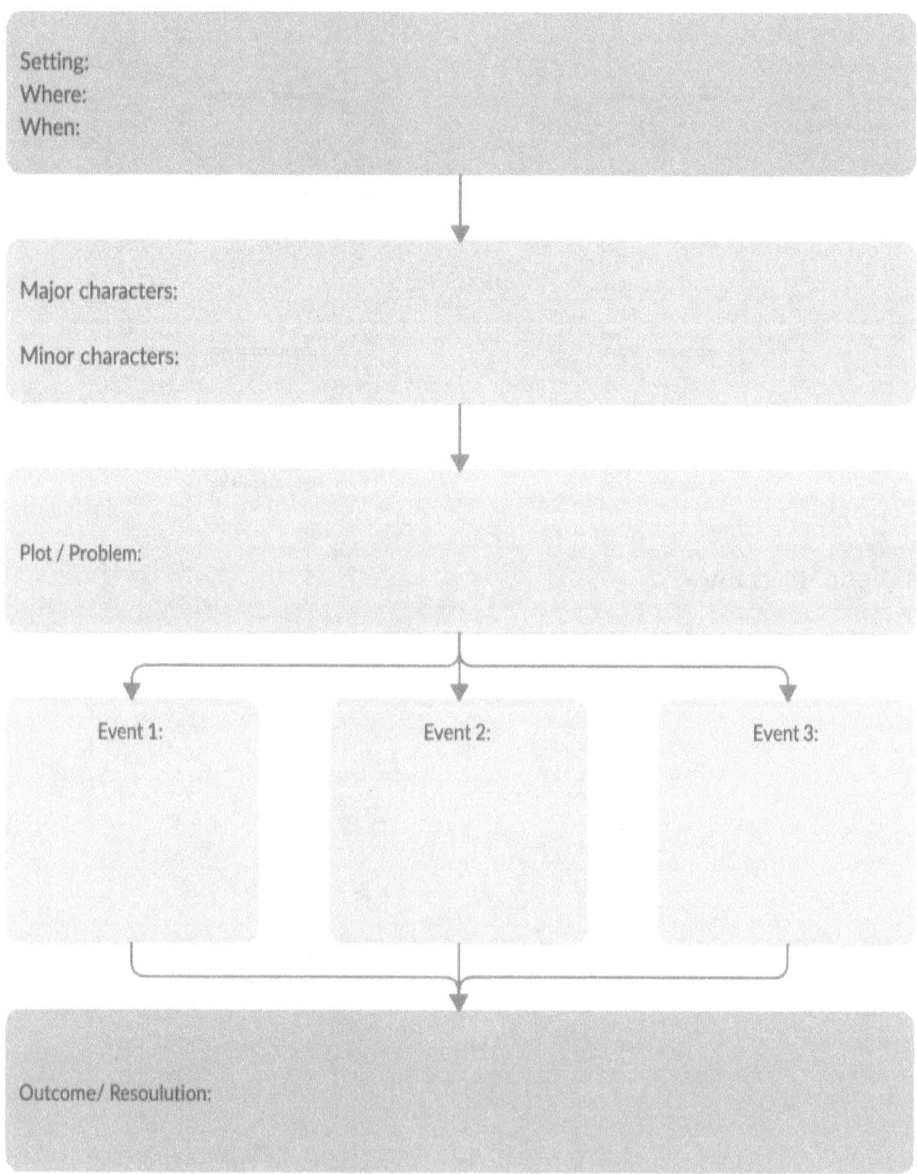

6.

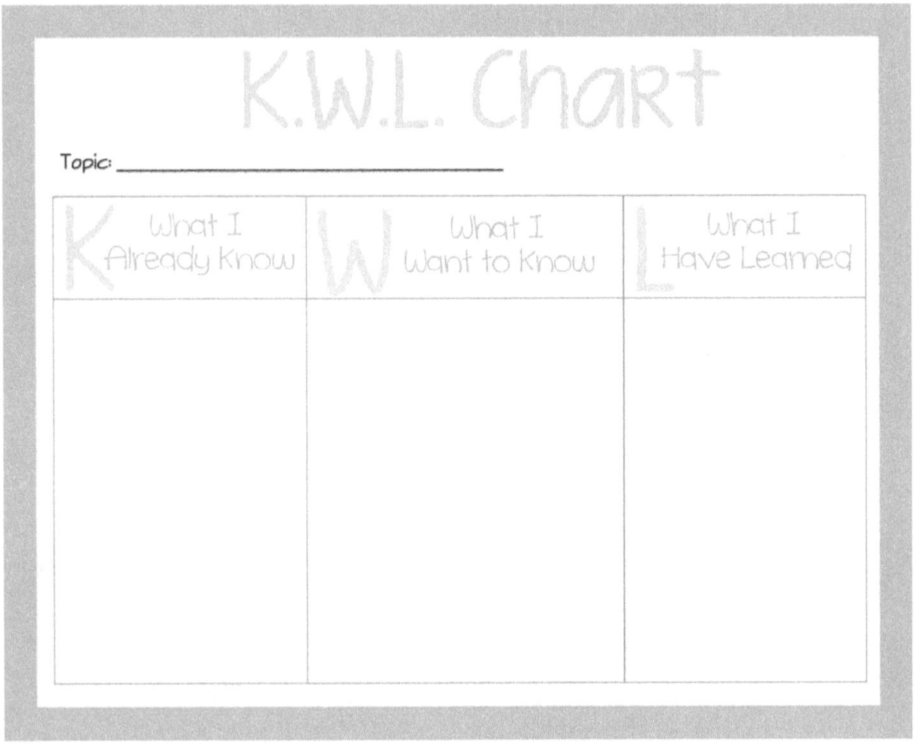

K.W.L. Chart
Topic:
K What I Already Know
W What I Want to Know
L What I Have Learned

7.

Cause
Cause
Effect
Cause
Cause

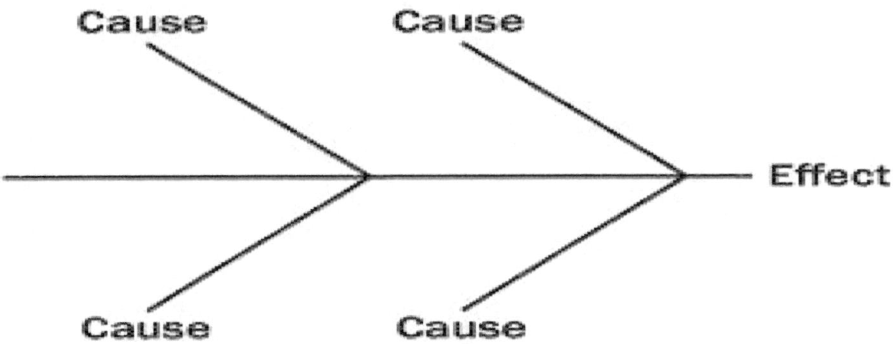

8. Spider Maps

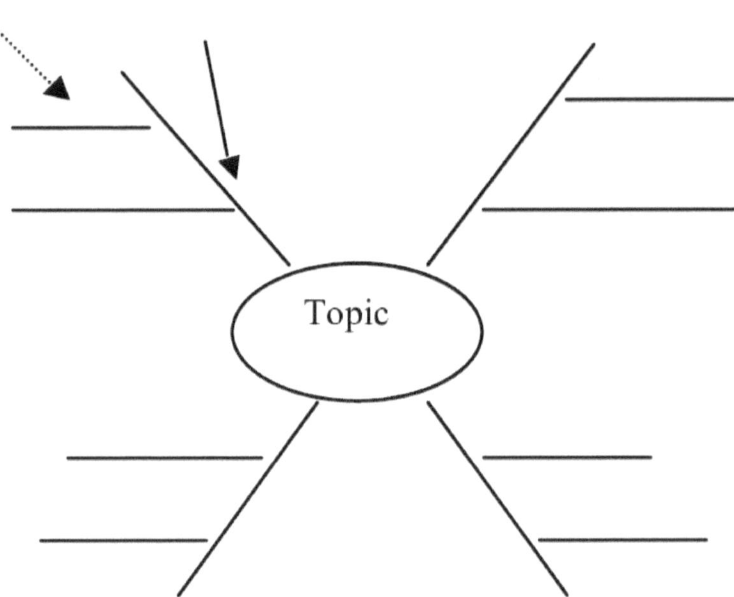

9.

T-Chart

T-charts are a type of organizer that lists two facets of a topic. They are used to either compare two items or contrast two items.

CHAPTER 28

EVALUATION AND FEEDBACK

Creative writing is a unique form of expression that varies greatly from person to person. Unlike grammar, which often has specific rules to follow, creative writing is a canvas for individuality, reflecting a child's thoughts, experiences, and imagination. Each child's journey in creative writing is distinct, influenced by their personal growth, environment, interests, and exposure to reading.

Teachers play a crucial role in assessing and nurturing this creativity. They must approach evaluation with a keen understanding of each child's writing level. This involves considering factors like their vocabulary, sentence structure, storytelling ability, and the depth of their ideas. Additionally, understanding a child's environment—cultural, familial, and societal—can provide insights into their perspectives and influences on their writing style.

When setting expectations, it's vital for teachers to tailor them to each child's capabilities and growth trajectory. Expectations should be challenging yet achievable, considering the child's current skill set and potential for improvement. By factoring in a child's reading habits, educators can gauge their exposure to different writing styles, genres, and literary devices, which can significantly impact their own writing abilities.

Crucially, a child's progress in creative writing is best measured in relation to their own prior work. Tracking their development based on their earlier pieces allows teachers to appreciate their individual growth, identify areas for improvement, and celebrate their achievements. This approach encourages a focus on personal advancement rather than comparing them to their peers, fostering a supportive and encouraging learning environment.

In essence, evaluating and setting expectations for children's creative writing requires a holistic understanding of the child—acknowledging their uniqueness, considering their environment and reading habits, and nurturing their individual progress as they evolve as writers.

> **Evaluation and Feedback.**

- Setting correct expectation
- Every child writes differently
- GPPS- Grammar, Punctuation, Paraphrasing and Spelling
- Structure and format
- Creativity and originality
- Give suggestions and feedback
- Follow through

Basis of Teacher Intervention

- Be on the same side as the child
- Write with the children (Then you know the problems with your question, time management, problems children face and why this happens)
- Share the marking scheme /rubrics
- Make it a win-win situation (you should get information on your teaching and they should be able to get a share of a lot of samples from peers)
- Teach and practice before you test (discovery by sample, discussion, doing and testing)

- Articulate exactly what you want from a piece of writing. (specific rubrics that the child understands completely)
- Empower children to assess – autonomous child (rubrics and peer checking helps with this)
- Every writing session must be followed by a feedback session.

The art of productive assessments

- Corrections must not be a mere judgement passed on performance.
- Segregate those who need personal attention and remediation.
- Ideally, give a collective-feedback to the whole class. No names. Include all kinds of samples – good, average and struggling.
- Keep the samples as your teaching bank. This gives you immense resources.
- Empower children with the knowledge of why an error is harmful. (This is important as then they will correct themselves faster if they know how serious it is)
- Give evaluated papers a personal touch. Encouraging remarks like I'm with you. I got your back. We will make it together. These are more helpful than could do better.
- Bright children also need remarks on how to get to the next step towards perfection. (Do not neglect them with a halo effect mark. They will have areas that can be bettered. If you cannot see it, ask someone to help)

Readings and Resources

- https://www.teachthought.com/pedagogy/20-simple-assessment-strategies-can-use-every-day/
- https://www.cmu.edu/teaching/assessment/assesslearning/index.html
- https://www.ispringsolutions.com/blog/8-ways-to-assess-online-student-learning

- https://www.edutopia.org/comprehensive-assessment-introduction
- http://www.ascd.org/publications/books/197171/chapters/The-Types-of-Portfolios.aspx
- https://www.thoughtco.com/student-correction-during-class-how-when-1210508
- https://m.busyteacher.org/15517-correct-student-error-writing-speech-how-when.html

Basic Writing Rubric

Feature	4 Strong	3 Developing	2 Emerging	1 Beginning	Score
Ideas	Establishes a clear focus Uses descriptive language Provides relevant information Communicates creative ideas	Develops a focus Uses some descriptive language Details support idea Communicates original ideas	Attempts focus Ideas not fully developed	Lacks focus and development	
Organization	Establishes a strong beginning, middle, and end Demonstrates an orderly flow of ideas	Attempts an adequate introduction and ending Evidence of logical sequencing	Some evidence of a beginning, middle, and end Sequencing is attempted	Little or no organization Relies on single idea	
Expression	Uses effective language Uses high-level vocabulary Use of sentence variety	Diverse word choice Uses descriptive words Sentence variety	Limited word choice Basic sentence structure	No sense of sentence structure	

Conventions	Few or no errors in: grammar, spelling, capitalization, punctuation	Some errors in: grammar, spelling, capitalization, punctuation	Has some difficulty in: grammar, spelling, capitalization, punctuation	Little or no evidence of correct grammar, spelling, capitalization or punctuation	
Legibility	Easy to read Properly spaced Proper letter formation	Readable with some spacing/forming errors	Difficult to read due to spacing/forming letter	No evidence of spacing/ forming letters	

Narrative Writing Rubric

Criteria	4 Advanced	3 Proficient	2 Basic	1 Not There Yet
Main Idea & Focus	Skilfully combines story elements around main idea Focus on topic is profoundly clear	Combines story elements around main idea Focus on topic is clear	Story elements do not reveal a main idea Focus on topic is somewhat clear	There is no clear main idea Focus on topic is not clear
Plot & Narrative Devices	Characters, plot, and setting are developed strongly Sensory details and narratives are skilfully evident	Characters, plot, and setting are developed Sensory details and narratives are evident	Characters, plot, and setting are minimally developed Attempts to use narratives and sensory details	Lacks development on characters, plot, and setting Fails to use sensory details and narratives

Organization	Strong and engaging description Sequencing of details are effective and logical	Engaging description Adequate sequencing of details	Description needs some work Sequencing is limited	Description and sequencing need major revision
Voice	Voice is expressive and confident	Voice is authentic	Voice is undefined	Writer's voice is not evident
Sentence Fluency	Sentence structure enhances meaning	Purposeful use of sentence structure	Sentence structure is limited	No sense of sentence structure
Conventions	A strong sense of writing conventions is apparent	Standard writing conventions is apparent	Grade level appropriate conventions	Limited use of appropriate conventions

Expository Writing Rubric

Criteria	4 Displays Evidence Beyond	3 Consistent Evidence	2 Some Evidence	1 Little/No Evidence
Ideas	Informative with clear focus and supporting details	Informative with clear focus	Focus needs to be expanded and supporting details are needed	Topic needs to be developed
Organization	Very well organized; easy to read	Has a beginning, middle, and end	Little organization; needs transitions	Organization is needed
Voice	Voice is confident throughout	Voice is confident	Voice is somewhat confident	Little to no voice; needs confidence
Word Choice	Nouns and verbs make essay informative	Use of nouns and verbs	Needs specific nouns and verbs; too general	Little to no use of specific nouns and verbs
Sentence Fluency	Sentences flow throughout piece	Sentences mostly flow	Sentences need to flow	Sentences are difficult to read and do not flow
Conventions	Zero errors	Few errors	Several errors	Many errors make it hard to read

FEEDBACK OF THE PARTICIPANTS WHO HAVE ATTENDED OUR CREATIVE WRITING TEACHER TRAINING PROGRAM.

The participants came from diverse work areas. All related to the field of education and I was fortunate enough to share my learnings with them. Here's what they had to say about my Training Program-

1. Such a wonderful workshop I have ever joined in. I Learnt plethora of new things and techniques from you,mam. Thank you so much for teaching and sharing with us.

– Nikita S

2. Thanks to mentor Priti mam who made the course more interesting. Now my understanding is much clearer when it comes to writing essay and stories.

– Swati Maheshwari

3. The flow of teaching was amazing and perfect..

– Sapna Gandhi

4. Learned a lot from this workshop. I got direction in the right way and got better idea about how to teach creative writing.

– Avni Chheda

5. Priti has in-depth knowledge about how to make things more interesting, I learned about how to bring a change in child's thinking and writing.

–Jigna Salia

6. Well designed with lot of efforts and conducted so well...hatts of to Priti mam.

Today's session was so well planned and so comprehensive, Learnt many nuances of story writing...

If I had known this as a kid I would have certainly become a writer.

– Dipti Dedhia

7. Thank you Priti mam for sharing your knowledge and enlightening us with new perspectives of writing. You definitely changed my viewpoints on many things personally and professionally. Filled with immense gratitude that I enrolled for your program. Thanks so much mam

– Anuradha Shetty

8. Also thank you Priti mam for your amazing mentorship, you are a true guide to English language and I look forward to more courses with you in future for sure to groom myself as a better English teacher.

9. I am very much clear now with differentiating Different topic otherwise actually wasn't able to differentiate Report writing & story & speech, descriptive, narrative how is it different. I thought for the first time about 5 senses & using it over a topic & thinking about it

– Ekta Nagda

10. First of all thank you very much for this Course. You made it so easy for me to understand and enjoyed every class. Five Sensory part was new for me. Creative writing Part is more interesting.

– Chetana Gori

11. I think the overall session was really insightful and the example that you used, the videos, the resources which you are very very useful. I learnt a lot of new things. I usually focus ongrammar, so the creative part is a little different. I had knowledge of idioms but not narrative writing and descriptive writing. I learned a totally new aspects of Creative Writing

– Jyoti Advani

12. Thank you Priti ma'am for your amazing mentorship, you are a true guide to English language and I look forward to more courses with you in future for sure to groom myself as a better English teacher.

– Vaishali Mehta

13. Thank you mam. It's been a beautiful journey of learning and sharing.. my debt of gratitude to you for organizing such interesting and interactive sessions.

– Ami Shah

14. Feedback for our program's content

- The course content is the ultimate level. one can learn the very basics of creative writing. It was an eye- opening program for me.
- The content and the resources provided are valuable and practical.

15. New learnings, quality content, fantastic handouts for future reference. Honestly, it exceeded my expectations!!

– Manjusha Kollara

16. Teacher training program is very well designed, explanations for every topic were excellent,assignments were brain storming and overall a good learning platform for me.

– Vinita Naik

ACKNOWLEDGEMENT

I would like to express my deepest gratitude to the mentors who have played an instrumental role in shaping this book. Your guidance and wisdom have been invaluable throughout this journey, providing me with insights that have enriched the content and elevated its quality.

I am indebted to the vast array of resources procured from the internet, which have served as a wellspring of knowledge and inspiration. The online community, with its wealth of information and diverse perspectives, has been an essential companion in the creation of this work. Special thanks to the individuals and forums that generously shared their expertise and experiences, contributing to the depth and breadth of the ideas presented in these pages.

Additionally, I want to extend my appreciation to the workshops I attended, both in-person and virtually. These learning experiences were transformative, offering practical skills and methodologies that have directly influenced the development of this book. The knowledge gained from these workshops has not only broadened my perspective but has also contributed to the practical application of the concepts explored within these pages.

Furthermore, I extend my appreciation to the authors of the books that I have referred to make the content of this book comprehensive. It has provided a solid foundation for the concepts explored in this book.

In addition, I would like to acknowledge the support of my family and friends, whose encouragement and understanding have been a source of constant motivation. The assistant teachers of my academy who helped a great deal with researching the content.

Last but definitely not the least, all my dear students who have been part of this teaching and learning, which has given me invaluable insights to be put in this book.

This book stands as a testimony to the collaborative spirit of the intellectual community, both online and offline. Your contributions, whether through mentorship, online resources, or published works, have been a cornerstone to this endeavour. Thank you for being an integral part of this literary voyage.

ABOUT US

PriNeel English Academy instituted in the year 2020 with the aim to provide high-quality language learning experience to student of all grades.

We create a supportive and engaging learning environment, where we empower students to develop their language skill.

Our mission is to help students of all ages to improve and enhance their English language skills. Our goal is to make every child confident learner. We are committed to ensure consistent growth in language skills of the child that go way beyond classroom.

Programs we offer:

E3 – Enhancing and Enriching English.

A holistic language development program to strengthen your child's core concepts and boost their confidence in English language.

It focuses on

1. Functional and foundational grammar
2. Creative thinking and writing
3. Vocabulary enhancement
4. Reading and comprehension
5. Journaling
6. Regular assessments and feedback.

CREATIVE WRITING HUB

1. Write Express

   Our year-long creative writing program aims to equip the children to understand the nuances of creative writing. It empowers the children to take their writing from blah to brilliant.

2. Creative Writing Club

   This club fosters and strengthens the love for creative writing and gives an opportunity to the creative cubs to explore a variety of form and genres.

3. Creative Writing Workshop

   A fun and engaging sessions, which help children to not only understand what creative writing is all about but also fall in love with the process of creative writing.

Academic Literature and language

For grade 7 to 10 (CBSE/ICSE/IGCSE)

- Effective study resources with extensive practice
- Personalised Attention
- Continuous Assessment with regular feedback
- Guaranteed growth graph
- Optimum batch size for focused learning

Creative Writing Teacher Training

A 6-days intensive program aims to empower teachers, tutors, parents to teach creative writing to children in the right way.

It offers:

- Structured curriculum
- Ample resources and lesson plans

- ➤ Session Recordings
- ➤ Certification
- ➤ We have been running this program successfully since October 2022 and have completed 8 batches of training and empowering educators.

Workshops and Seminars

We conduct numerous workshops and masterclass for children all-year round to ensure value-addition apart from their regular learning.

We invite industry experts and resource persons who bring their expertise and contribute to the holistic development of the child. It enables the child to explore new avenues like story-telling, public speaking, etc.,

Connect with us:

Call – 9819641436

Email – prineel2020@gmail.com

Instagram – Prineel_academy

Blog – learningsandsharings@blogspot.com

www.ingramcontent.com/pod-product-compliance
Lightning Source LLC
Chambersburg PA
CBHW021422150726
47989CB00001B/80